BlockChain Cryptocurrency and Ethereum

Learn Fast!

What You Need To Know To Make Money In An Hour

3 Manuscripts in 1

By
Daniel Reed

I0492687

Blockchain: Learn Blockchain Fast! – What You Need To Know To Make Money In An Hour

Cryptocurrency: Learn Cryptocurrency Fast!: What You Need To Know To Make Money In An Hour

Blockchain: Learn Blockchain Fast! – What You Need To Know To Make Money In An Hour

Introduction

I want to thank you and congratulate you for purchasing this book, *"Block Chain/Crytocurrency – Learn Fast! - What you need to know to make money in an hour"*.

This book contains proven steps and strategies on how you can make use of the blockchain technology. Within this book are all the details that you need to fully grasp how blockchain works and how you can mine bitcoins or ether by being part of a blockchain network.

The blockchain is the revolutionary technology that is believed to change the way people do transactions online. By learning how this technology works and how you can use it, you will be able to take part of one of the biggest innovation today and get an insight on how the world's future online transactions will be.

I hope you enjoy it!

Chapter 1 - What is Blockchain?

A blockchain, on a surface level, functions like the Google spreadsheet that you may use on a regular basis – people can write on it, and you can keep track of all the changes that are made among the users who has the permission to edit it. You may think of your spreadsheet as a very important tool that keeps all your data in check and can be updated on a regular basis.

Today, most of the transactions that you do daily is stored on a company's database – your online purchases, social media entries, blog uploads, etc. needs to be kept in a secure server so that you can keep track of what's happening to them. However, you know that the world is not a perfect place. It is always possible for a server to go down, crippling thousands or even millions of online consumers that will not be able to access a data or service that they need. It is also possible for irregularities to happen in-between transaction. That makes every consumer want a system that they can easily check and would be secure enough for all their transactions to never be tampered with for anyone's gain.

The blockchain technology promises to do all that by keeping a decentralized ledger of transactions, that allows everyone access for the right checks and balances. When implemented across industries, this technology will change the way you think about security and transparency.

The Database that Everyone Will Love

The blockchain technology is essentially a piece of software that aims to consolidate data into a one big chain of events. Its aim is to make sure that data is stored in a chronological manner and that there is no way for transactions that are stored in it become changed. It also makes it a point that everyone can see the flow of transaction. Compared to normal ledgers, you cannot make erasures on this ledger – once a piece of information is already confirmed, it cannot be taken out anymore.

You can think of the blockchain as a Lego set that is made of data. Within a box set, you could get different pieces and then connect them together and they will fit perfectly. However, you would want to create a certain design, so you would want to fit the blocks together in a certain manner. However, once you put the pieces together, it would be impossible for anyone to take them apart – you can only add to the chain of blocks that you have already created, but you cannot take out a piece.

Think of the usual database – when you do one transaction after the other, you expect them to follow an order so you can easily validate if all the information is there. However, databases that people usually use can be easily changed or even lost – they are either stored in a facility that can easily be accessed, or someone working from the inside of the facility can steal or tamper with them. Now, what if everyone that has a computer can have access to those databases? Everyone will easily find out if something is changed in someone's copy because their own copy of the data will tell so. Also, everyone should agree whether a certain addition to the database is acceptable or not, based on rules that everybody agrees on.

By decentralizing data, or making everyone privy to information, you can trust that there is no one out there that will singlehandedly destroy data or make unwanted changes on it, thus making the distributed information very secure. Also, by having a system that tells whether a certain set of data is valid or not, the system is not likely to be rigged by an individual.

What makes it even better is that it can to accept transactions from numerous parties, as long as they are involved in the chain of transactions. It doesn't matter where you are in the world – if you do a transaction that belongs to a certain chain, then your data can be stored securely in this electronic ledger. Compared to most databases that exist today, you can include your information in a blockchain without having to sign up for a third party's service.

To sum it up, blockchains are the solution that everybody needs to prevent data manipulation, and there are a lot of benefits that will stem from that. By solving the issue of data manipulation, everyone can enjoy a more transparent and accessible data management without having to rely on any third party to do that job. What people can expect soon are transactions that are faster and more secure.

Do Blockchains Exist Now?

Yes, there are blockchains that are fully functional right now. One of the most popular blockchains is the bitcoin, which is a cryptocurrency that can be used to buy goods and avail services. Since the bitcoin is maintained by a blockchain, you can actually see all the transactions that involves a bitcoin, which includes the transaction done in order to produce the first bitcoin, and how people send money to others. When you go to www.blockchain.info[1], you can actually see a graphical interface that shows you the entire chain of transactions done using this currency.

There is also a blockchain that is dedicated making decentralized applications, which means that there are people that are starting to make some services available to people without a single company owning managing the use. This means that when successful, the applications that they are creating will never suffer from outages, making them more stable than programs that run on private servers.

There are also blockchains owned by private organizations that are created to make their own private database secure by taking advantage of the tamper-proof quality of data storage that the blockchain offers.

The blockchain technology is also starting to get rolled out on many banks and legal firms, essentially to maintain the integrity of their records and confirm transactions faster than they used to be.

Blockchains Will Free the Way People Transact

Blockchains are created in such a way that it would change the way people create transactions and trust services that they want to avail. It is de-

---

1.   http://www.blockchain.info

signed in a manner that solves most of the people's issues when it comes to creating transactions with virtually everyone in the world, no matter where they are. By making this technology possible, everyone can have the freedom that they want to enjoy when they make exchanges and use platforms that are available to them.

Blockchains are thought to impact world's processes more than what the internet did to the postal service. It is bound to change almost everything that you can do that involves internet connectivity and is predicted to affect everyone who uses smart devices and computers. Its functions are also thought to affect everyone that accesses and processes data with a massive chain effect to the point that it will disrupt every industry that involved the use of data.

Chapter 2 - How Blockchain Works

You can think of the blockchain as a very large spreadsheet available on your Google Drive. However, changing even a single entry on that spreadsheet would require a very special permission: it cannot be edited unless everybody that has access to that spreadsheet agrees to the changes that are proposed to be made. However, the only change that they can do to it is to add additional data, which will still be approved by everyone that is within the group.

What is the Blockchain Supposed to Do

At this point, you know that blockchain is essentially a software that is designed to work like a shareable Excel spreadsheet, only that it is more secure.

All transactions that make use of the blockchain are guaranteed safe, because a blockchain does not rely on any third party to run or maintain its ledger, it relies on a blockchain network. This network makes use of a protocol based on consensus, which means that the majority of those that belong to that network needs to agree that the contents that are going to be added to it are legitimate. Furthermore, those that belong to the blockchain network makes it a point that all transactions are secured by using hashes and the transaction owner's digital signatures.

Consensus is achieved because everybody in the network has the exact copy of the transaction. This means that if there is anyone that wants to tamper with a single transaction will have to find a way to make changes to all copies that are spread all throughout the world. What makes security in a blockchain even better is that all those transactions that are added into the blockchain are hashed using the SHA256. The SHA 256 is an algorithm that is designed to create a one-way encryption. Once a transaction is encrypted, there is virtually no way for one to decrypt it back to its original form. For this reason, no one in the network really knows what the transaction that they are trying to validate really is from, making all transactions anonymous.

Ensuring Legitimate Transactions

If all transactions in the blockchain are anonymous, how does one make sure that they are done by a legitimate person that is capable of holding their end of the bargain? This is solved by enforcing the use of the digital signature, which ensures that all people that are doing exchanges within the blockchain are legitimate users and not mere imposters.

At the same time, digital signatures also add another layer of security by making use of private keys in a very public ledger. While all things that are happening within the blockchain community are already secured by their hashes, people also need privacy. You can just imagine what will happen if everybody knows that you have a certain amount of bitcoins (which, today, is a lucrative currency to have). By also encrypting information about transaction owners, everybody will have the peace of mind about their personal data.

Chapter 3 - Difference Between Blockchain and Bitcoin

You have probably heard about bitcoins if you are reading this. Or someone might have mentioned about it and you became curious.

What is a Bitcoin?

The bitcoin is a cryptocurrency that was introduced in 2008. During that time, Occupy Wall Street made strong statements against the alleged manipulation of giant financial corporations of the economy – misappropriation of funds, outright fraud, overcharging, you name it. In an essence, the bitcoin currency is introduced as an attempt to solve all problems that a centralized form of money management has – it aims to get rid of the consumer's need for an intermediary, the need to pay for transaction fees, and to make sure that all transactions that involve money are transparent. The bitcoin has created a decentralized economic system wherein consumers can freely choose who to send their money to and know what exactly takes place when they store or spend it.

The bitcoin has grown exponentially since the time of its introduction. It used to be only used in underground transactions, but now, almost every industry makes use of it. You can even include fintech giants such as Visa, Mastercard, and PayPal among its users.

A Closer Look at Bitcoin

Bitcoin, just like every currency out there that you can use, can be used for exchanges because it has an ascribed value. The only difference it has from fiat money is that it is a virtual currency – it is not represented by anything tangible, but the technology enables you to use it for exchanges. As a form of cryptocurrency, you can use this to buy goods or avail services.

If you have a bitcoin and you make transactions, the blockchain network will send the person who will be receiving your funds an encrypted code, which will contain the necessary information that will verify your identity. It will also tell the other party that you have enough funds to cover the transaction. The other party will decrypt the transaction's code using a program and will then receive your bitcoins.

Is the Blockchain the Bitcoin?

The bitcoin makes use of the blockchain technology, but no, they are not the same. The bitcoin does possess the qualities of the blockchain, which are the following:

• Irreversible

Once a transaction using bitcoin is confirmed, there is no way for this to be reversed. Since it works on a decentralized structure, there is no one out there that can help you cancel or make changes to your transaction.

• Pseudonymous

Bitcoin transactions are never connected to real-world personalities – there is no one in the world that will know how you are spending or receiving bitcoins over the network. To receive bitcoins, you send people a public bitcoin wallet address so they will know where to send the cryptocurrency. However, that public address is different from your private key, which adds another layer of security to your private details.

Because all transactions are hashed on the blockchain network, you can only analyze the flow of transactions in a blockchain network. However, it is impossible for you to connect a person to a bitcoin wallet, especially if you are looking at the entire bitcoin ledger online.

• Fast and far-reaching

If you do any transaction over a bitcoin network, you can expect your transaction to be processed within minutes. That's right – you do not wait for hours to send or receive payments, compared to traditional payment systems that you use which make use of third party processors. What's more is that the bitcoin network is indifferent to location – sending money to a person that lives in another continent is just as fast as sending funds to a person next door.

• Secure

Just like all other transactions that make use of the blockchain technology, a bitcoin transaction is encrypted with a one-way hash, which is virtually impossible to decrypt. This makes all transactions done using a bitcoin tamper-proof.

• Permission-less

The software that you can use to do transactions using a bitcoin is free – that means that the application that you can use is not developed by a third party that will charge you for transactions or tell you whether you can send money or not to a different person. No one can prevent you from transact-ing with anyone using your bitcoins.

Mining Bitcoins

If you want to start getting your hands on some bitcoins and you want to buy them, then you have probably heard about bitcoin mining. Bitcoin mining is essentially the way people controlling nodes, or computers that are participating in verifying bitcoin transactions, create new bitcoins for the network by confirming transactions in the blockchain network.

This means that by mining, transactions within a blockchain network are secured and locked into blocks. This is done by solving the nonce (also known as number used only once), which is based on a cryptographic prob-lem that is based on the SHA 256 algorithm. This compensates those who are spending resources to confirm transactions and to generate new bit-coins to spread around.

Chapter 4 - Benefits of Using Blockchain

While the blockchain is extremely popular in running cryptocurrencies such as bitcoin, this technology can interrupt the way several industries operate. Because blockchain is designed to free several industries from a lot of limitations, this revolutionary technology might just replace many organizations that you are so used to dealing with daily.

Introduction of the Trustless Exchange

One of the main goals of the blockchain is to create a world where there is no middleman. This greatly reduces third-party risks.

More Efficient Transactions

Once this technology is adopted by several industries, transactions can be done faster because they do not have to be confirmed by any centralized organization. Transactions done over the blockchain network experience less risk of not being confirmed or processed since they are not likely to experience downtime, compared to transactions that are needed to be stored or process. Since consumers don't have to avail a centralized party's services for their transactions to push through, they also avoid high transaction fees.

Empowered Users

Without having to conform to the rules of intermediaries that approve transactions, everybody will have the freedom of controlling their transactions. At the same time, people will also have the ability to monitor all activities that concern their transactions.

Data Security and Reliability

Decentralized networks that process and store data makes all transactions secure – since the blockchain does not rely on a single physical network to process and store user information, it is not likely to come to a halt and delete information that it already contains. Within the same vein, blockchains are also virtually impregnable – it would be impossible for anyone to decrypt its one-way hash or attack all the computers that are storing blockchain data, which makes it more capable of withstanding attacks.

Integrity of Processes

Once a blockchain is designed to perform tasks in a certain way, there is no way for someone to change its protocols. Because of this, you can always be certain that transactions do not skip a process or become altered while being confirmed.

Simplified Ecosystems

Because all transactions that are done within a blockchain are stored in a single ledger that everybody can view, organizations that use it does not have to deal with having to create multiple ledgers or databases. Everybody can rely on a published ledger in order to keep track of data.

Chapter 5 - Disadvantages of Using the Blockchain

The blockchain technology is a work in progress. At this point, several technologies are still being developed to make sure that it does what it needs to do, which is to make its users perform transactions without the risk of their data being compromised. Despite all the promises that the blockchain aims to deliver, no one can say that it is perfect.

To some, blockchain exists as the utopia for financial technology and other industries that it aims to changes. However, there are still plenty of challenges to be addressed.

Shaky Regulatory Status

If you are thinking of investing in cryptocurrency, making sure of its legality in your region is necessary. Right now, there are certain areas that prohibit the use of the bitcoin for exchanges. Because the blockchain is still a technology that is still under development, there is a possibility of dispute about existing regulations on how transactions will be processed and how this technology may replace existing processes that still work for the consumers.

The Challenge of the Network Size

While the blockchain is created to withstand attacks, being impregnable would depend on the size of its network. That means that if this technology will not gain the participation of computers in a variety of locations across the globe, then it becomes possible for attackers to find out where the nodes or computers that are confirming the transactions are. While it is easier to penetrate centralized servers, a network that is too small is still very possible to attack.

Speed and Cost

Having a decentralized mode of storing and processing data may seem to be ideal, if the system is already matured. However, blockchain networks are still relatively new and the nodes that are working to confirm transactions may not be enough to process all transactions that happen in a day. As of this writing, combined networks working for the bitcoin blockchain can confirm 243,623 transactions within 24 hours. Visa, one of the fintech giants in the world, can confirm 150,000,000 transactions every day. Looking at this numbers, it looks like the bitcoin blockchain needs a lot of work when it comes to improving transaction speed.

At the same time, now is not yet the time when bitcoin transactions are affordable for the middle-class consumer. Bitcoin transactions become more expensive, depending on the amount of storage space they occupy, and the current norm is that transactions that have higher transaction fees get prioritized. The average transaction fee, as of this writing, would cost around $2.45. However, transactions that have this fee usually gets confirmed after an hour or a day.

Risk of Human Error

If you are going to use a database that doesn't easily allow you to make changes, then you need to make sure that all the entries that go there are of high quality. While there is nothing you can do to alter the contents of the transactions (which gives you the idea that the system is secure), you need to have all the checks and balances to ensure that all entries that enter the ledger are accurate.

Mining Consumption

There is a reason people get paid for solving the cryptographic puzzle to confirm transactions – mining bitcoins and confirming blocks can be costly. Combining the electricity consumption and hardware costs can be too much for an ordinary PC owner. While the logic for the requirement for miners to have Proof of Work is to make sure that making changes to a transaction is as difficult as adding a transaction to a block, miners are also doing the same task to solve the nonce first, which does not really make the confirming network very efficient.

For this reason, many blockchain developers are switching the method that their coins can be mined and how transactions can be validated. Certain blockchains, such as the Ethereum and the Peercoin are making the big switch from Proof of Work to a greener and more viable way of making their nodes work to confirm blocks.

Scalability Issues

At this point, the blockchain being used by bitcoin can push for seven transaction confirmations per second. However, there are doubts if all blockchains will be able to have a capacity to confirm more transactions. At this point, the blockchain has a peak capacity of 56,000 transactions per second, but for the amount of transactions that needs to be confirmed across the globe, it still needs to scale to accommodate more and enhance blockchain services.

Blockchains aim to resolve this by encouraging more people to join their network to confirm transactions by incentivizing participation. With the hopes of getting more nodes to participate in validating transactions and making changes on the way they can be confirmed, more developed blockchains are aiming to solve this issue in the very near future.

The Possibility of the 51% Attack

The blockchain network confirms that a transaction should push through based on consensus. This means that at least 51% of the confirming computers should agree that a transaction is valid before it pushes through. This way, people can trust that the blockchain is secure in such a way that there is no single point of vulnerability that could collapse its entire structure.

However, there is the possibility of the 51% attack, or a possible "rigging" of results by a more dominant sector of the confirming network. Those that are in favor of the blockchain think that this type of attack is not close to reality, but there are cyber security experts, such as Kaspersky, that argue that this is still likely to happen given the norms of mining nowadays.

Proof of Work, which is essentially having to spend electricity, hardware, and time for a computer to guess the cryptographic puzzle needed to confirm a block (and earn bitcoins in the process), is the reason blocks of information get attached to a blockchain. However, what miners aim to do nowadays is not to confirm transactions but to hoard the bitcoin. When this happens, the bitcoin is not distributed across the worldwide grid – those that are able to afford spending for energy consumption and the rig will end up controlling the bitcoin mining game. When you think about it, there are numerous fintech giants that can readily avail the machinery for mining. Visa, for example, is upping their game by investing in hardware and consumption that will allow them to confirm transactions in seconds. To date, China is the country that is leading in producing and using bitcoin mining rigs. With mining nodes concentrated to certain countries or corporations, rigging the mining game for a 51% attack becomes a huge possibility.

Because this flaw has already been predicted, several alternative blockchains and their cryptocurrencies are making some changes on how transactions can be verified and how their currencies can be spread along their grids.

Would Blockchain Evolve to Defeat Challenges?

The blockchains that you know now are probably not the blockchains that you will be using in the future. The bitcoin blockchain, for example, is still at an incredibly young age – it is rough around the edges, but it shows where improvements should happen. Being able to understand how the blockchain can improve will allow this technology to be the promising data structure that people want it to be.

Chapter 6 - The Blockchain and the Finance Industry

The financial system across the globe works to serve billions of people in a day, and moves large sums of currency in the process. However, the traditional financial setting faces numerous challenges, which include arduous paperwork, document mismatch, exorbitant transaction fees, plus numerous opportunities for fraud.

While the current financial system seems to work on the surface, Pricewaterhouse Coopers (PWC) reported that about half of today's intermediaries that serve the financial sector suffers economic crime annually. That means that all the institutions that you currently trust to secure and process your financial records and transactions, which include money transfer third parties, payment services, and even stock exchanges, are compromised one way or another. The current solution for intermediaries to continue providing trust is to increase regulatory costs, which is of course transferred to consumers like you.

The financial system makes use of processes and technologies that may be antiquated – when everything fails, people will be forced to go back to paper-based transactions that are vulnerable to error and manipulation. At the same time, it is also centralized, which makes it vulnerable to system attacks or technical difficulties, which brings back the consumer to the hassle of the first scenario. Also, it is extremely exclusionary – it essentially denies billions of consumers the very tools that they need to ensure that transparency is in place. The proposed solution for all these, as you may have already thought of, is the blockchain.

The Best Way to Do Exchanges

You already know that blockchain can give birth to cryptocurrency, such as the bitcoin, but that is only a small part of what this technology can do. With blockchain, it is possible for you to do asset exchange in a secure manner, thanks to cryptography, the digital signature, and network consensus. On top of that, it enables two individuals to make an agreement and do an exchange without knowing each other, but still trust that they are dealing with a legitimate entity that can hold their end of the bargain. All these are done without having to rely on a middleman to verify identities and permit the transaction to happen.

What Will Happen to the Banking System?

Right now, banks are the ones that are going to be disrupted the most by this technology if they do not do the necessary upgrades. For this reason, many financial giants are starting to invest in blockchain solutions, which provides them the benefit of reducing cost and friction with intermediaries that they also use. Because banks can easily process transactions on their own without having to rely on third party solutions, the use of blockchain may lower the cost of banking. While they are not keen on replacing the fiat currency with cryptocurrency, the banking system can definitely benefit from what this system has to offer.

Known intermediaries, such as Visa and Mastercard, are also jumping in into the blockchain investment as well. In the future, you may expect more fintech giants promoting services that make use of this ledger system.

Most experts say that genuine disruption of the blockchain to the finance industry is yet to happen in a decade. You could probably imagine financial transactions that are free from data manipulation, human error, and high cost would happen within seconds. Right now, the fintech side of the blockchain is still under development; however, the above promises are the things that you can count on.

Chapter 7 - Blockchain and Other Industries

While financial services are the first ones to employ the blockchain system, other industries are also bound to improve when they use this technology. Even without having to delve with cryptocurrency, other industries will also benefit from incorporating blockchain into their processes.

Healthcare

Digital signatures that are present in data stored in blockchains will promote the privacy and availability of health records. At the same time, using blockchains and ensuring that medical facilities, insurance companies, and health practitioners are part of the blockchain will drastically reduce instances of fraud in this industry.

Government

Government offices can definitely benefit from blockchain when it comes to expediting exchange of information between departments, which is bound to improve government services. Through blockchain, government offices can also make sure that data is released in real time in order for certain policies to be enforced in a timely manner. This will greatly affect government actions that are time-sensitive, such as emergency responses.

Blockchain will also impact fact-checking because it will make a more transparent means for citizens to access government transactions and fund allocation. In its very nature, blockchain will combat corruption across government offices and push for transparency in public documents and available services.

Law

Blockchains prove to be capable of storing huge amounts of information, which will include contracts. Smart contracts, or protocols that make sure that what is stated in the contract is the only action allowed in a particular blockchain, will affect how contracts that are already agreed upon by two parties can be fulfilled. Because smart contracts will force agreements to be met, no one will have need a law practitioner to act as a middleman. For example, you would not need a legal firm to ensure that you are going to be paid a certain amount when you submit a project to a client.

Energy Industry

The power generation business can benefit from the blockchain's ability to register alternative means to generation. By employing a smart contract, people will be able to find a way to get credits for alternative energy that they will be able to provide.

It's a good thing that energy producers and consumers have already found a way for them to directly transact with each other, without having to rely on giant third parties that will tell them where they can get their energy from. Right now, the startup TransactiveGrid started using the Ethereum (you will know more about this later) in order to make it possible for producers and consumers to transact directly in a peer-to-peer manner

Crowdfunding

Right now, crowdfunding relies on intermediaries, such as Kickstarter and Gofundme, in order to have platforms where they can raise funds for projects or startups. While the known platforms make it possible to enforce trust between project makers and their supporters, they do cut a huge percent of the funds that are going to be raised.

This scenario will change once blockchain enters this industry – project creators will be able to find a way to provide tokens as rewards to their backers, which they can exchange for goods or services at a later time.

Online Media

If you are an independent artist and you want to come up with a way to get payment directly from your listeners, then blockchain is your friend. Blockchain will enable you to sell and license your music without having to rely on platforms such as Spotify, which will take a cut from your earnings. At the same time, blockchains also provide a more efficient cataloging system for those that produce and distribute online music, which makes it easier for fans to discover you.

Just like in the music industry, all other types of media will benefit from the low costs of transactions, which means that applications in the media industry can process transactions without having to pay fees. It also broadens up the options that consumers can enjoy when trying to access media online. For example, a website that runs a magazine can start charging their readers on a per-article basis, instead of having to lock them for an entire month.

Voting

Blockchain offers a smart solution to prevent fraud in voting, thanks to its efficient identity verification and smart contracts which will ensure that only legitimate entries are counted for polls. Of course, once a vote enters the system, it cannot be changed or removed without having to disrupt the entire network of computers that operate it.

Communications and the IoT

One of the biggest strengths of the blockchain technology is to support anything that exists on the internet that involves transactions. This will drastically improve coordination in the Internet of Things (IoT), which will allow multiple devices to coordinate more seamlessly.

Hospitality and Travel

Businesses that cater to consumers by offering travel and hospitality services can enjoy a much-simplified system of settlements. At the same time, blockchains can even support loyalty points systems that most businesses in this industry offer – it can speed up the process of points verification and offer rewards without delay.

Credit and Reputation

By having a distributed database that caters to reviews, people and businesses can enjoy trustworthy endorsements without having to rely on third parties to do the survey for them.

The Supply Chain

Consumers can enjoy better transparency on how the products they consume are created with a decentralized system that will display all transactions that transpire from the manufacturer or farm to their households. When the blockchain is widely-adopted by different consumer markets, you will no longer have to be concerned about the origins of the products that you purchase – all you would need to do is check the database for verification.

Your Industry

If your industry needs to store data and requires security and transparency, then it can definitely benefit from implementing the blockchain technology. Blockchains will also offer you the opportunity to speed up certain processes that you may be implementing right now, thanks to decentralization. In the future, you may expect most of the businesses and organizations that you are transacting with to be adopting a system that close-ly resembles a blockchain, or fully adapt this technology.

Chapter 8 - Ethereum and Other Cryptocurrencies

Bitcoin might be the trendsetter when it comes to cryptocurrencies, but it is not the only cryptocurrency out there. As of this writing, there are more than 900 virtual currencies that exist and are actually being mined and used for exchanges all over the world. You can expect this number to grow over time.

Cryptocurrencies, such as the Bitcoin, can be created by anyone that has the ability to mine and sell them to the public to be used for exchanges. Just like fiat money, such as the dollar, these virtual currencies have value that goes up and down depending on their scarcity and utility.

Of course, it is also important to remember that cryptocurrencies are designed to power the blockchain that they are running in. Knowing them equates to knowing what kind of blockchain they serve and what this blockchain aims to achieve in its creation. Within this chapter, you will learn how blockchains could transcend the goal of merely replacing the fiat currency when doing financial transactions, but also change different industries that are still running on the traditional and centralized structures.

What other cryptocurrencies are making it big in the market right now? Here are the virtual currencies that are making waves across industries.

Peercoin

Peercoin's goal is to become secure and decentralized without making its blockchain's network spend a lot in order to make it grow. Its distinguishable feature is that it provides an annual incentive for those who have it, and that it is not very strict on the number of coins that will be available on the market.

This cryptocurrency is thought to be the solution for possible sustainability for the cryptocurrency. While it is currently being mined using the Proof of Work system, it is making a transition to Proof of Stake, which is a system that will make way for new coins on the system without having to invest too much on energy consumption.

Current price: 1 PPC = 1.23

Market cap: $29,862,334

Nxt

Nxt advertises itself as one of the second-generation cryptocurrencies, which means that this cryptocurrencydoes not concern itself with having to function as one of the standalone currencies out there, but to provide a true decentralized platform for exchanges that are happening online. The creators of this currency don't focus on just hitting the goal of becoming a large currency, but to actually create a sound economic ecosystem online. For this reason, people may recognize the Nxt as a platform for online exchanges or a marketplace rather than an actual currency.

One of the great features of Nxt is that it offers its users the option to "shuffle" their coins, which means that those who are exchanging using Nxt coins have a way to obscure their transactions and gain anonymity.

Current price: I NXT = $0.062792

Market cap: $62,729,604

Namecoin

Namecoin is one of the revolutionary cryptocurrencies out there that goes beyond being involved in mere financial transactions. Being one of the early alternative cryptocurrencies out there, this cryptocurrency is powering a P2P technology for verification that makes it possible for people to create websites that are not reliant on popular servers.

Compared to most of the cryptocurrencies out there, the Namecoin is not designed to increase its price – it is actually programmed to make people enjoy lower transaction fees when they try to get a domain for them to join a decentralized internet. This allows future webmasters to enjoy a blockchain that is designed to make it easier for them to create websites without the high cost of acquiring domain names and getting their content on a server.

Current price: 1 NMC = $1.24

Market cap: $18,326,482

Factom

Factom is one of the cryptocurrencies that enjoy a huge market. Known for using a blockchain that is designed to create immutable databases for corporations, the blockchain behind it is designed to create a database that is stored in the Factom blockchain, which is then hashed and stored into the Bitcoin blockchain. Right now, the people behind Factom are working on also adding the Factom hash into other large blockchains for an extra layer of protection to their users.

Factom's current clients include China's smart cities. For a continually growing currency, it is making quite a smart move to offer their technology to governments for streamlined services and data security.

Current Price: 1 FCT = $19.98851064

Market Cap: $174,801,564.3

Litecoin

Litecoin is dubbed as the "silver to the Bitcoin's gold". What makes it special is that it is widely used by independent contractors and that it involves a script (aptly called scrypt) that makes mining impartial to those that have more advanced mining hardware. This cryptocurrency is widely accepted by developers, but the number of merchants that accept this is also growing in number, making it one of the virtual currencies that is worth investing in

Current price: 1 LTC = $ 48.0946294

Market Cap: $2.54 billion

Zcash

Zcash was one of the younger cryptocurrency that has a lot of promise. Zcash defines itself as the https of the Bitcoins http and boasts of better privacy and selective transparency among its users. In Zcash, all transactions are still recorded on the blockchain, but it keeps more sensitive information such as the amount, sender, and recipient more private. What makes it even better is that users that make use of this cryptocurrency has the option to make transactions that are "shielded", which allows users to make use of the zero-knowledge proof (ZPK).

Current price: 1 ZEC = $172.859861

Market Cap: $ 268.91 million

Dash

Formerly known as the Darkcoin, this cryptocurrency is considered to be the most anonymous currency – while it works on a decentralized network like other currencies, it also runs on a mastercode network which makes transactions very hard to trace.

Current price: 1 Dash = $250.144451

Market cap: $1.89 billion

Ripple

This cryptocurrency boasts of instant, sure, and cheap international payments, which makes it a great alternative to current money-sending options. It has a ledger that does not make use of mining, which makes it very different from most cryptocurrencies out there. Since this currency does not need to be mined, it drastically reduces the network's need to use electricity and ensures that the confirming network experiences less latency. Instead, Ripple works to provide incentives to those nodes for their behavior. Ripple targets to distribute the currency to those businesses that need to make up for tighter payment spreads.

Current price: 1 XRP = $0.1817744

Market cap: $6.96 billion

Monero

If you are gunning for an untraceable, and ultimately private and secure, currency, then Monero will be something that you will be interested in. This cryptocurrency grew out of community participations and is donation-based and has a strong focus on growth and decentralization. Its blockchain works with the use of the ring signature, which is designed to shroud the real participant among a "ring" of signatures – since all the cryptographic signatures are designed to appear valid, it would be hard to trace which is the real one.

Current price: 1 XMR = $ 98.7014872

Market cap: $1.4 billion

Ethereum

The Ethereum is one of the cryptocurrencies that are growing fast, and according to Coinbase.com, it is the forefront of the cryptocurrency. The reason is simple – the blockchain behind it is designed not just to secure transactions, but to allow freedom in creating possibilities through apps.

The Ethereum is designed by scripting languages that are, compared to the Bitcoin, very unrestrictive. Instead on focusing on transfers and securing exchanges, the Ethereum introduces the bleeding edge of cryptocurrencies by welcoming the developer community to create decentralized apps, or dapps, which are designed to follow their design. What makes the Ethereum blockchain extremely functional in decentralizing exchanges is that it is dedicated to creating applications that will allow more possibilities online, making transactions that you probably never thought of to be possible. The secret sauce behind it is the development of applications that actually doesn't need any third party to run, which makes a lot of sense in the very goal that the blockchain technology aims to achieve.

Current price: 1 ETH = $256.019334

Market cap: $24.22 billion

Introducing the Proof of Stake

While the Bitcoin is mined through Proof of Work, the Ethereum will eventually grow and get scattered around the globe through Proof of Stake. While both types of transaction validation aim to achieve a distributed consensus among the network, The Proof of Stake determines who will create the new block on the blockchain in a mode deterministic manner – those that have already participated in the Ethereum blockchain gets chosen, and that chosen one does not get a reward.

What makes the Proof of Stake an awesome way of validating transactions? Proof of Work is not necessarily an environmentally-healthy way of mining for cryptocurrency. Mining for a block on the Bitcoin blockchain takes a lot of energy. How much energy is that? One transaction requires the amount of electricity that could power almost 2 American households. A block is a group of transactions, and that is a lot of energy consumption in total. This is not just unhealthy for the environment, but could be unhealthy for the economy as well since electricity is being paid for by fiat currency.

Under the Proof of Stake mining system, people are compensated by transaction fees instead of a substantial reward. Participants that want to validate transactions are those that actually have an Ether, while the Proof of Work system makes anyone with the ample computing hardware and can afford electricity join the mining venture. By keeping those that are already supporting the Ethereum blockchain, stakeholders are invested in validating transactions in a conscientious way. After all, it is their economy that they are trying to build.

Dapps and the Participation of the People

How will the Ether get spread around if no one really gets an incentive for mining? The most logical answer for this is involving people in dapp projects. Right now, most of the dapps are in the beta stage, wherein their developers are encouraging people to join them, in exchange of tokens or Ether. Developers are also able to spread around Ether and app coins as payment for transactions that they do with other developers or dapp users.

App tokens are very interesting because it allows several Ethereum projects to get launched and become maintained without even having to rely on any venture capitalist. Some dapps that have gone live now were able to raise more than $250 million by simply creating app tokens which has the following characteristics

1. Tokens are the currencies that can be used within the app where they are created. You can think of them as the gold coins that you earn in a computer gam which, of course, can only be spent within the game. However, if you need more access, you can actually purchase them using fiat currency or another cryptocurrency that has value.

2. Everyone that contributes to the growth of the app is compensated by tokens. That means that when you contribute, you gain more access to the features of the app or get more tokens.

3. Tokens work like other cryptocurrencies – the more people are likely to use it, the more expensive they get. Moreover, you can convert them to any currency, depending on the value ascribed to it.

One classic example of a dapp that has made it big thanks to its own coins is Stork, which is a file storage application. There is no central figure that operates it and runs solely on the blockchain network that power. The Storjcoin is created as the application's currency that allows its users to buy storage space.

What makes app tokens lucrative in a sense is that you can actually hold on to them until they go up in value, then convert them into a different currency of your choice.

This brings up a whole new dimension when it comes to making money in the world of blockchains. Creators of dapps are incentivized when their creations become a success, and people that are already supporting them get a share of wealth by trading the coins that they already have. This creates a win-win scenario in the dapp scene, since this will inspire other developers to invest in another developer's creation and also create an application that will be very useful to the community in order to get the support that they want in order to succeed. Since this business model creates an atmosphere that is very independent, every developer has a chance of actually creating a successful project even if they have limited budget.

Chapter 9 - Beginners Guide to Investing in Cryptocurrency

Having read the previous chapter, you might be thinking that you want to have a time machine and travel back to 2011 when Bitcoin seems like a shrouded experiment that is very cheap to invest in. However, investing in cryptocurrencies is definitely not for the faint of heart – it takes certain knowledge in order to make a smart investment.

Why Invest, and Why You Shouldn't

Besides what you have read so far, there are only three reasons why it is wise to invest in any form of cryptocurrency:

1. You want to protect yourself from the fall of the Dollar, which people assume to happen at some point in time
2. You actually support the goals that lead the cryptocurrency to what it aims to create, which is a free world that enjoys a free market
3. You understand what blockchains are and you actually like technology.

However, you need to keep in mind that there are also some bad reasons that you may already be thinking of (and are influencing you) when it comes to investing in a virtual currency. First, if you think that you are just falling to the hype of making quick money with this, then stop. If there is something that is telling you that you want to spend all your resources to buy cryptocurrency while you can still afford it, then you may be better off doing something else. Keep in mind that you should always learn what you are getting into before you even spend a dollar in a currency that you will not be able to touch.

One of the things that you need to remember is that cryptocurrencies function in order to support the goals of the blockchains that they operate in. More than just having a value in your currency, you may want to invest in them simply because you will need them to take advantage of what their blockchain's technology has to offer.

How Are You Going to Get Them?

The easiest way to get cryptocurrency is to buy them. If you are interested in buying a Bitcoin, for example, you can go to an exchange site such as coinbase.com and use their online wallet to store your purchase. Another site that you may want to check out is the coinmarketcap.com

You can also opt to mine the currencies by participating on the blockchain network that is running the cryptocurrency that you are eyeing. Mining would involve having to spend on hardware and electricity in order to confirm transactions, but this can become a very lucrative source of passive income once you have everything set up and running. However, you can only do this on cryptocurencies that are powered by the Proof of Work system.

You can also grow your digital money by doing staking, which is essentially the Proof of Stake version of mining. You may get different rewards by doing this, but it would need less physical investment compared to mining using hardware and electricity.

Another method of getting cryptocurrency in your wallet is to do arbitraging. Arbitraging is essentially the buy-and-sell method of acquiring and selling cryptocurrencies that you can get your hands on in order to get cash out of them and to grow your portfolio as well.

Review the Alternative Currencies

In early 2016, the Bitcoin practically has the entire cryptomarket for itself. However, that is not the case now, as you have read in the previous chapter. Nevertheless, there are hundreds of other cryptocurrencies out there, and you may want to invest in those that actually cater to how you want to spend them, and not just their current worth.

How would you know whether a cryptocurrency is worth investing in? There are three main factors that you need to consider:

1. The currency's trading volume and its market capitalization

Market capitalization refers to the amount of value ascribed to all the coins of the cryptocurrency available in circulation. When the market capitalization of the cryptocurrency you're eyeing is high, that can mean two things: it's either people are really putting value to the currency or there's a lot of it available in all markets that it is participating in. For this reason, you will also need to pay attention to its daily trading volume. If the trading volume is high on a daily basis, then it means that it is widely used in transactions, which is an indication of a healthy economy.

1. The currency's verification method

The verification method is the one that would really set cryptocurrencies apart. As explained earlier, the verification method is the process wherein a blockchain system agrees on whether a transaction is valid or not, and is also the way the cryptocurrency is generated and spread among members of the network.

1. Acceptance

Just like fiat currency, a cryptocurrency doesn't have any use if other people are not willing to buy it from you or if you cannot exchange it for any goods or services. For this reason, it is always best to invest in cryptocurrencies that has a healthy market that is welcome to use it for an exchange.

With these things in mind, you may want to ask yourself the following questions:

1. Do you think that your investment is safe with the development team?

Time to remind yourself of the first rule of investing: always make sure that your capital is preserved. At this point, you may want to do some research when you are going to buy a currency or store your virtual money in your wallet. Do you want to leave your hard-earned money with a development team that has been hacked in the past? Did you read that they were involved in a scam? While the coin that they are offering might grow in the future, you may want to think twice before investing with them.

1.   Does the currency that you want to invest in has a long-term plan?

Again, more than being exchanged into cash, you may want to think about what the currency is trying to achieve in the first place. Most cryptocurrencies disclose their white paper, and if you have not read it yet, then it's high time that you do so. Is this cryptocurrency capable of achieving their project goals? What would the project that they have in mind look like in 10 years? Asking yourself this question will help you recognize a cryptocurrency that will grow in value.

If you think that the cryptocurrency that you're eyeing is just great at marketing but has no backup plan when things don't go their way, then you might just be investing in an ICO that has a great website but is not capable of delivering.

1.   How long are you going to stay with the currency?

If you are after monetary gain, it pays to know which coins will be great to flip in order for you to enjoy their short-term benefits. When you acquire a currency or plan to do so, set your personal expectations and your exit price.

For more detail on crypto currencies keep reading further in this book.

Chapter 10 - The Future of Blockchain

Blockchain is predicted to be as massive as the internet now – it is predicted to take over most, if not all, of the transactions that you are capable of doing now. Moreover, it will change the way you think about data and security.

At this point, people are just beginning to see what blockchain can actually do, thanks to current innovations that have gone live. However, think of it as the internet in the 1980s – back then, the concept of World Wide Web is intimidating, and transactions are infuriatingly slow. However, people were quick to see that it would revolutionize two aspects of the human condition: communication and education. In the end, it boils down to letting people access what they normally cannot in the status quo.

Blockchain achieves to do the same in different ways – in about ten years, this technology will change institutions, starting from the goal of freeing consumers from third parties that mediate exchanges. This goal, in itself, already changes a lot of things.

Apart from people actually having direct access to information, they will also have a free hand over creating and expressing themselves. This immediately disrupts a number of processes that people do in their daily lives. With the possibility of dapps, people can be as innovative as they can get within a blockchain's system. Internet is also unlikely to be regulated anymore. Because there is no single point of failure, blockchains predict a future where no task is left undone.

It does not mean though that all blockchains are perfect. It pays to always remember that they are designed to rigidly store the information that has already been approved by its network. While decentralizing decision making may be ideal in so many levels, there are also circumstances in history wherein the majority could be wrong. At the same time, it also does not mean that the majority can not be manipulated.

However, it pays to understand that the blockchain that you may know now is arguably not the blockchain that you will know tomorrow. It is possible that the Bitcoin will not be the largest cryptocurrency in the market and could be replaced by an unknown alt coin that you may not be even aware of today. It is possible that this technology may even prove to be negatively deconstructive in certain industries. After all, the blockchain is as only good as the program that it is built on, and the success of every platform built on this technology would depend on its participants.

Right now, there are too many speculations about the impact of the blockchain – it might sound too good to be true, but this might be the utopia that people are clamoring for, thanks to its ability to give power to multiple persons to make decisions and have control over its functions. However, this also means that responsibility and accountability is also dispersed to many different levels in a network. At this point, people may argue that individuals may not be ready for this kind of personal responsibility and freedom.

The Takeaway

In the end, the blockchain lies on the people's ability to take control of their future without having to rely on systems that may exist today. Just like any large innovation, the blockchain provides people a more direct access to their needs, allowing them to be more empowered in creating technologies that will make personal development possible.

However, the blockchain is still a work in progress – its process and its ability to fulfill the promise of being independent and free from manipulation is still under development. At this point, you and the other people who already know a thing or two about this emerging technology are its beta testers that are likely to encounter bugs while it is being slowly rolled out.

But this does not mean that the blockchain will fail at what it promises to do – the more you involve yourself with projects that already use it, the more insight you will have on how things could actually turn out in the future. If you want the blockchain to succeed and deliver, you will need to be part of its development team today.

Cryptocurrency
Learn Cryptocurrency Fast!: What You Need To Know To Make Money In An Hour

Part I What Is Cryptocurrency

Chapter 1 - The Rise of Cryptocurrencies

On a cool balmy Sunday afternoon on September 14, 2008, executives of Bank of America and the British bank Barclays had some bad news for Richard "Dick" Severin Fuld Jr., Chairman of Lehman Brothers, the giant Wall Street investment bank. They informed a sullen Fuld that they were pulling out of talks to save Fuld's once esteemed institution – there just wasn't enough money, assets, and shareholder support to prop it up. It was a conclusion that seemed unimaginable - Lehman Brothers founded in 1870, was considered one of the most stable financial institutions in the world.

The next day, Lehman Brothers announced that they were filing for bankruptcy protection – which began the process of its eventual liquidation. Lehman was the biggest institutional bust in the 2008 worldwide financial crises, which led to trillions of dollars in losses for everyone; individuals and companies; big or small. The Dow Jones Industrial Average lost over 500 points during the day, wiping out billions in public and private wealth.

About a month later, a shadowy recluse named Satoshi Nakamoto published a paper on The Cryptography Mailing list at http://www.metzdowd.com/mailman/listinfo/ cryptography[2] describing what he termed a new digital currency. Less than three months after releasing the paper, "Bitcoin: A Peer-to-Peer Electronic Cash System," Nakamoto released the initial digital currency software and issued the first units of the new cryptocurrency which he called Bitcoin.

Many asserted that the timing of Nakamoto's release of this software and the issuance of the first bitcoins were a response to the financial meltdown. Others argued that the while timing was just a coincidence, it seemed that the world had lost its trust in not only the financial institutions that precipitated the crises, but also in the governments that were supposed to be the watchdogs to prevent exactly what happened in the 2008 meltdown.

---

2.   http://www.metzdowd.com/mailman/listinfo/%20cryptography

Apart from the massive monetary and assets losses, the biggest loss during the crisis was the loss of trust by people in their long revered and respected institutions. In the blink of an eye, the assets of many Americans sank under the groaning weight of unsustainable debt. Mortgage debt greatly exceeded the values of their houses, stock losses ravaged their retirement funds, and as companies closed down, loss of incomes created a vicious cycle of financial and economic desperation. But perhaps the most chilling aftermath of the crises was what happened to "basic" money.

For investors, the closest thing to putting currency under the mattress was investing in money market funds. These funds are where businesses "park" their overnight cash, and while it earns practically nothing in terms of interest, it is at the very minimum, supposed to retain its value. However, on Wednesday, September 17, the world woke up to find out that these funds had lost almost $150 billion on the aggregate. Going back to the mattress analogy, it was like waking up and finding out that the $100 that you had the night before was now just $99, which meant that someone had "stolen" money from your otherwise safe mattress.

The U.S. dollar, the most stable and reliable store of value, was on the brink of collapse, and the world of money and currencies as the world knew it, seemed like it was teetering on the verge of collapse.

Some people like Satoshi Nakamoto while feeling betrayed, did not take things lying down. Instead of sulking and regretting personal financial losses, they began working hard for a new stable monetary world.

Chapter 2 - Cryptocurrencies vs. Currency

<u>Currency</u>

Before I describe what cryptocurrency is, it would be useful to quickly describe what that dollar bill in your pocket is, or currency. Currency is a paper, metal, or electronic representation of a "medium of exchange" which facilitates the exchange of goods and services between parties. Currency by itself (paper or metal) has little or no value, especially in its electronic form, when you pay someone online through your bank phone app or website, for example.

Currency's value comes the fact that it was issued by a national government, for example, the United States, which guarantees its face value after it prints the money and distributes it to the public. Governments in this case are "Trusted Parties," acting as a middleman in facilitating this exchange.

Currency can also be transferred and paid on the internet. You can transfer money or pay for bills using the internet, or some third-party payment or remittance service like Western Union. A few strokes on a keyboard are all that's required. You can also pay through credit and debit cards, transferring electronic currency from our deposit accounts to these cards.

This sounds like a great arrangement, and it usually is. For more or less stable governments like the United States and most Western European countries, the U.S. dollar and the Euro are "trusted" stable currencies, and no one would think twice taking them as the form or payment for anything.

Now consider two scenarios where the typical currency model might fall apart. There are many countries whose governments are not quite as stable or reliable, at least from a currency standpoint unlike than the U.S. or countries the European Economic Community, which share the Euro. These governments have unstable political structures and are be run by despots and irresponsible officials who either use their country's treasury as the personal wallet, or have no idea how to manage their countries' finances including their currency. The worst thing they can do aside from stealing the money is to print so much of it that the value of the money drops like a rock, because of so-called "hyperinflation."

For example, imagine that you go to sleep planning to spend $10 to buy a gallon of milk, a loaf of bread, and a can of SPAM the very next morning. When you go to the grocery the next day, you are told that all your $10 can buy now is a stick of gum. The government that you trusted has just suddenly reduced your purchasing power and diminished your lifestyle! This is what happened for example, in Zimbabwe under President Robert Mugabe in 2007-2008, where prices doubled every 24 hours for several days.

Or consider a woman in an impoverished country like Afghanistan, who was using a bank branch in the capital Kabul to withdraw cash and pay for her groceries. But a suicide bomber blew himself and five others on August 29, 2017, removing her only source of money. In a flash lost the ability to use currency to pay for her necessities.

In these cases, the "Trusted Parties" of Zimbabwe and Afghanistan could not guarantee the safety and access of their citizens' money. When the value of money falls below what it is expected to be or you cannot get to your money at all, a safer and more convenient alternative is both needed and required.

There are also hundreds of millions of people that live in "underbanked" and unbanked countries worldwide, where there are no current banking or currency systems to facilitate commerce. In the United States, we take it for granted that we have bank accounts and access to spending power whenever we need it. However, the story is different in many places around the world. Africa is a glaring example where some countries unbanked population represents up to 90% of their population.

Enter cryptocurrency.

<u>Cryptocurrency</u>

The best way to define cryptocurrency is by describing its features. While it is still a medium of exchange in the currency sense of the word, it possesses very different qualities from the currencies that we have been used to.

First, the "crypto" in cryptocurrency comes from the word cryptography, which is simply, writing and interpreting code. Cryptocurrency was and is created by creating computer code and assigning ownership and value to this code. *Like any other currency*, paper or otherwise, it has "value" because people assign it value and more importantly, people THINK that it has value, despite the fact that all it is is a bunch of zeros and ones digitally assembled into monetary values.

The first major cryptocurrency, Bitcoin, was created in 2009 by a series of complex mathematical formulae that were run on computers with at the time, possessed significant processing power. Because it apparently removed the shortcomings of other attempts at creating cryptocurrency in prior years, its value was established as legitimate. People added value to it because they started to believe that like paper money, it could be used as a common medium of exchange for goods and services.

Second, because of cryptographic sequences and processes, it is not possible to duplicate a cryptocurrency unit once it is "created". This is like the serial numbers on a dollar bill, except that dollar bills, like all paper currencies, can be counterfeited or duplicated. A $100 U.S. dollar bill with a serial number of K01134564H for example, can be forged and "used again" depending on how many times it can be illegally copied.

This is not possible with cryptocurrency, because of multi-ledger approach, coding and mathematical probabilities, which will all be discussed later, make it impossible to do so. This prevents what is called, "double spending," an undesirable situation which is equivalent to using counterfeit paper currency.

Third, an important aspect for most cryptocurrency is that there is a limited number of unites that will be produced. Nakamoto, the Bitcoin founder, set a cap on how much Bitcoin can ever be generated, 21 million, until the year 2140. After this date, no more new Bitcoin will be created. This is expected to add to the value of the cryptocurrency, because unlike currencies issued by national governments, there is no printing press that can create currency on a whim.

Fourth, there is no single "Trusted Party" in a cryptocurrency network like a central bank in a national government maintaining a national currency. Because a decentralized system of verification, coding, transaction recording, and ledger keeping depends on the consensus of hundreds of thousands, and maybe millions of cryptocurrency miners and coders, a cryptocurrency system's trustworthiness is probably unassailable.

An increasing band of people, most of which do not know each other, verify and validate the mathematical algorithms that are the backbone of a cryptocurrency system. Cryptocurrency software is "open-source"; nobody owns or controls it, and its design is public. More importantly, everyone who wants to take part in its operation can play a role in its operation.

This "openness" can also be considered a weakness by critics of the cryptocurrency system because since there is no central authority governing the issuance and use of the currency, there is also no fallback in case of theft, dishonesty, or losses arising from cryptocurrency transactions.

Still Nakamoto and his minions have apparently found the answer to having a reliable currency, which ironically does not rely on trusting any single person or persons.

Creating money – currency vs. cryptocurrency

As with any other currency created by a national government, there are two major aspects of managing and transacting in, the currency. The first is how the currency is made, and the second is how the currency is used. With the U.S. dollar, there are really two kinds of money – money in the form or coins and paper which we are most familiar with, and money in the form of bank deposits.

In creating deposits, the U.S. government "creates" money by selling government securities such as Treasury bonds and Treasury bills, and depositing funds to the banks' accounts. The banks, using a fraction of money deposited by their depositors as "collateral," lend money to individuals and companies, make investments, which increase the money supply in the economy. A portion of this, about 10% is issued in the form of paper currency and coins which only the U.S. Treasury can print out. Banks "buy" this physical currency from the U.S Treasury and in turn, issue them to the public.

With cryptocurrency, there is no central banking authority that issues any new funds or currency for spending by the general public. There are also no "middle men" such as banks who will facilitate the creation and distribution of the new currency. Cryptocurrency is created through the interaction of thousands, and perhaps millions of cryptocurrency "miners" who try to solve mathematical puzzles and formulae devised by a particular cryptocurrency's founders and software designers.

Using money – currency vs. cryptocurrency

There are two ways that currency can be used as a medium of exchange. The first and most common worldwide, is using physical coinage and paper money. The other is using electronic and digital means to use the money to transfer money balances from one account to another. In electronic transfers, there could be at least two more parties in a payment transaction aside from the payer and the payee. For example, look what happens when Alice has to use her bank to pay Bob $100 by transferring money to his bank:

Andy⇨ $100 ⇨Andy's Bank ⇨$100 ⇨Brenda's Bank ⇨ $100 ⇨Brenda

<—SUPERVISED BY CENTRAL BANKING SYSTEM—>

Somewhere along the way, either banks will collect a fee for the payment transaction. When Alice pays via credit card, there are also at least two more additional parties in the transaction: the credit card company and the bank that processes Alice's credit card. In this case, Bob will pay a transaction fee for the privilege of getting paid by Alice's credit card.

In a regular currency system, Alice and Bob rely on two or more external parties and on these external parties' systems. They assume that the banks and other intermediaries that handle their financial transactions are financially sound and honest. After 2008 and Lehman Brothers, this assumption was shaken at its very foundation.

In a cryptocurrency system, the payment from Andy to Brenda is direct, just passing through the cryptocurrency's mathematical algorithm network:

Andy⇨ $100 ⇨ MATH ALGORITHMS⇨ $100 ⇨Brenda

The independence from a centralized authority while an attractive feature of cryptocurrency is also its biggest drawback. There is no authority or central agency to go to when a problem arises. For example, some units of Bitcoin have been observed and reported to have just disappeared into thin air in the early days of Bitcoin's operation. There is no currently no mechanism yet available to address, much less fix, transaction problems that may arise from cryptocurrency transactions.

Part II   The Cryptocurrency Mechanisms

Chapter 3 - Cryptocurrency Functions and Components

At its core, CRTC is simply a digital file that lists various accounts and money just as a physical ledger would. A copy of this file exists on every node in the CRTC network. Note that if you are just sending and receiving money, or buying to selling using CRTC, you do have to maintain or monitor any ledger in the CRTC system. A person does not have to maintain a ledger just to use Bitcoin to send and receive money, this is for people who want to help maintain, and obtain "compensation" from the system.

In typical currency and monetary systems, the functions of currency creation, distribution, monitoring, and protection are vested in separate organizations, all of them under the watchful eye of regulators. In the United States, this would include the U.S. Treasury, the Federal Reserve, and the Federal Deposit Insurance Corporation, which insures bank deposits up to a certain amount. Under this umbrella are the individual banks, the credit card companies, and other various independent financial intermediaries such as Western Union, Xoom, and small neighborhood check cashing places.

In its own way, the currency system has been "decentralized" whereby you can pay for groceries at your supermarket check-out counter by swiping your card and make purchases online. The controls, custody, and processing of payments however, are still in the hands of the centralized powers.

In a cryptocurrency system, all the functions we described previously are carried out by a huge and growing network of users with a cryptocurrency system. While some enterprising entities have come up with ways to facilitate their processing, such as wallet and exchange systems, the functionality is still dependent on how this network of users behave in the aggregate. For the most part, in its less than ten years of existence up to this writing, the major cryptocurrency systems have worked with impressive reliability with very few glitches and problems.

All the functions of cryptocurrency creation, distribution, and acquisition are performed within that cryptocurrency's basic programming rules and the actions of its users. All of the users work in tandem and mostly in cooperation, to ensure that the cryptocurrency network functions properly. The discussions of various mechanisms in the following chapters, while appearing to be in some form of chronological order, are in fact, part of a system where the parts are all working the same time: cryptocurrency creation, acquisition, payments, transfers, and recording. In our "real world" where we are interested mostly in using cryptocurrency as money, the things that we will be mostly concerned about are wallets with their transaction keys; the transactions that travel across, and populate the network; miners, and of course, the consensus blockchain, the "ledger" linking that controls the system, and is the heart and soul of cryptocurrency systems.

The shows the various functions and features that are part of a cryptocurrency system. Before we dive into how transactions are processed, let us discuss the various parts of the cryptocurrency ecosystem.

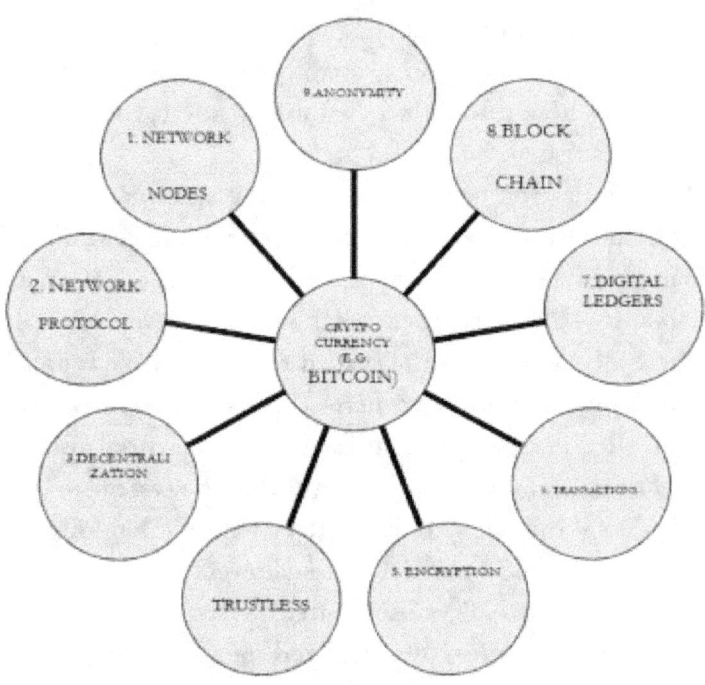

The Cryptocurrency Processing Network

1. Network nodes – A cryptocurrency system is comprised of a wide web of independent but cooperative "nodes" of users who comprise the buyers, sellers, and miners (those who work to get "newly issued" cryptocurrency units). Depending on the cryptocurrency (Bitcoin, Litecoin, Ethereum, etc.) these nodes, which represent individual consumer users can be in the tens of thousands.

2. Network protocol – This is the original "system" that was designed by the founders, creators, or inventors of a particular cryptocurrency. In Bitcoin's case, it is Satoshi Nakamoto and his (presumed) collaborators. It represents the rules, mechanisms, and code that runs the cryptocurrency. If you were building a road system, the network protocol would be the roads, the signage, and the signals. It is the basic programming code that comprises the structure and functionality of a particular cryptocurrency system. The network algorithms dictate how transactions flow, and especially how to obtain new units of the cryptocurrency if and when it is issued.

3. Decentralization – A cryptocurrency network is comprised of thousands of nodes, and there is also no one central authority to manage data flow. Cryptocurrencies are a peer to peer, distributed database – In a cryptocurrency system, there is no single place where all the data for the system resides. Unlike typical currency and banking systems where the information is stored and controlled in a central location, the data is stored and maintained by thousands of parties working within the system.

4. Trustless - The big problem with centralized banking institutions was, as the 2008 financial crises showed, that they could not be trusted. Satoshi Nakamoto wanted a system that required no trust in anyone, much less a centralized one. The computing problem that tried to solve was the so-called Byzantine Emperor's Problem, where you needed a system of numerous redundant checks and balances to make sure that all the transactions in the system are accurate and not subject to error or fraud. The blockchain system provides this system of checks and balances.

5. Encryption – Mathematical encryption is the basis of the trustless function. All transactions within the system are subject to heavy encryption and this is one of the attractions of a cryptocurrency protocol. Transactions are processed and approved using an approach where it is statistically impossible to introduce corrupt data, create duplicate information, and "steal" information. Together with the large distributed database, the encryption algorithms differentiate the system's security from others that need heavy security features.

6. Transactions – Consists of the transfer of funds between two parties. In a cryptocurrency system, this transfer is made between two or more digital "wallets" which house the currency. The other "transaction" that happens within the system is mining, where system members are able to obtain new cryptocurrency by solving complex mathematical and cryptographic puzzles.

7. Digital ledgers – This is where all the information of a specific transaction takes place. Each transaction and each ledger are singularly unique based on the encryption system, and these ledgers are available for everyone on the network to see, a feature that allows transactions to be verified and approved by the network of users. These ledgers are called public ledgers, because they need to be made available to all parties within the system.

8. Blockchain – This is at the same time the most important component and the most important function of a cryptocurrency system. It incorporates the trustless and encryption functions to facilitate the recording and verifying of cryptocurrency transactions. It allows the nodes to agree at regular intervals on the true state of transactions in a ledger. Blockchains comprise the unshakeable and solid foundation of the major cryptocurrency systems like Bitcoin. The blockchain has captured the attention of the computing world since Satoshi Nakamoto released his new currency, Bitcoin, in 2009. Many have called it the fifth evolution of computing because it has supposedly created the crucial missing "trust layer" on the internet.

9. Anonymity – The true identity of the founder (founders?) of

Bitcoin, Satoshi Nakamoto has never been revealed, nor does it look like it will never be. Anonymity is a pervading principle around a cryptocurrency network. Hashes and public and private keys, which we will be discussing shortly, replaces specific identifiers such as names and account numbers within the network, unless someone wants their true identity revealed.

Chapter 4 - Starting a Cryptocurrency Transaction

Before we go with the detailed discussion of a cryptocurrency transaction, let us have a high-level look at the cryptocurrency system. At its very core, the cryptocurrency ledger just lists accounts and money like a regular bank ledger. The big difference is that this file exists on every node or computer on the network. For example, a ledger like the following will exist in every node:

LEDGER

Andy	6.5
Brenda	7.25
Cal	.50
Denise	4.4
Edward	100.0
Fran	65.0

This ledger exists on each and every node in the cryptocurrency in the world:

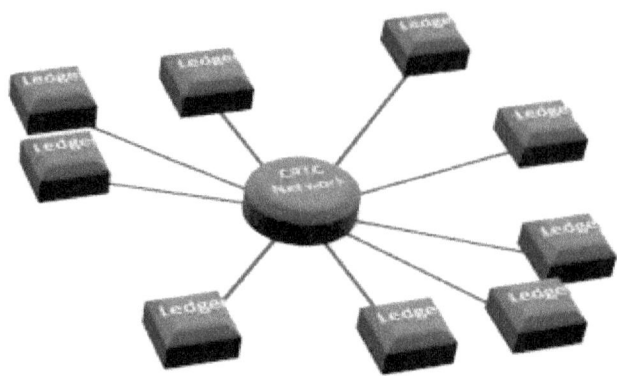

The numbers in the ledgers really do not represent anything physical in the financial world outside of the cryptocurrency system. They have value because the users have decided that they have value, and that they can use the currency to buy and sell real world goods and services. The United States Federal Reserve "created" U.S. currency many years ago, and let people believe that the paper and money and coins that they created were worth money (initially because of gold backing). The world of cryptocurrency has created the same faith and belief.

The figures and information in the ledgers possess value because the participants in the system believe that they digital currency has value. While the Federal Reserve has given us faith that we can trust the system to use the currency circulating around the world, in the digital world of cryptocurrency, the transaction histories represented in the ledger IS THE CURRENCY.

Detailed Sample Transaction

Let us begin our journey into the guts of cryptocurrency with a very simple example of how a cryptocurrency transaction works in real life by using a simple buy and sell transaction. For simplification purposes, we will use the abbreviation "CRTC" to represent the cryptocurrency that is being used for transactions.

Let us say that Andy wants to send money to Brenda, in this case 10 CRTC. Currently the ledger shows that Andy has 5o units, and Brenda, 10. He broadcasts the message to the network that says,

"Send 10 CRTC from Andy to Brenda."

The transaction will broadcast the information to all the nodes in the system:

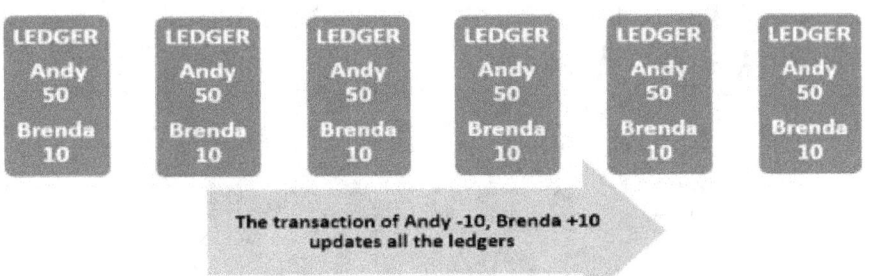

The transaction of Andy -10, Brenda +10 updates all the ledgers

Everyone on the network who wishes to maintain the system, will get a copy of transaction, and pass the transaction information on to other nodes in the system.

This ledger system sounds a pretty similar to the way any bank keeps a ledger. In this case, instead a single entity maintaining the ledger like a bank, a group of several nodes maintain the ledger and everyone in the CTRC network knows about each other's transactions. When the bank maintains the ledgers in a typical banking transaction, they are the "trusted party" in the whole system.

Each node who receives the initial broadcast will update their copy of the ledger and inform others to do the same. The question arises though:

"How can we be sure that Andy and everybody else recorded the transaction correctly?"

The solution is that the CRTC protocol requires a highly complicated form of password, called a digital signature, which is required for EACH transaction. As in a handwritten signature on a paper document, it provides the validity of the broadcasted transaction, but instead of a physical signature, the authenticity is accomplished via a complex mathematical algorithm called a cryptographic hash function, which creates a number combination that is impossible to figure out by guessing because of the number of combinations possible. This prevents tampering with addresses in the CRTC system.

For example, if Andy sends 10 CRTC units to Brenda, and 20 CRTC units to Cal, the transaction messages might look like the following (but in digital format):

> **Andy to Brenda – 10 CRTC units,**
> **Digital signature :**
> 00C146513233453453L322314630
>
> **Andy to Cal   –20 CRTC units,**
> **Digital signature :**
> 00C1655132334554724212344453
>
> The two digital signatures are different from each and every signature ever created, and will be created!

Why is this digital signature so special? Because of the impossibility of faking or tampering with a transaction. First, there are two components to this signature/password: a PRIVATE KEY and a PUBLIC KEY. The system for broadcasting digital signatures looks like this:

To create the transaction, a PRIVATE KEY + MESSAGES creates a signature.

Therefore to "spend" money, you have to prove that Andy is the real owner of a public key address to where the funds was sent. This is symbolized the following cryptographic function (f is the function that generates the signature):

$$\text{SIGNATURE} = f\,(\text{MESSAGE, PRIVATE KEY})$$

To verify that Andy is the owner of the public key, the cryptocurrency network will take the digital signature together with another message in a different function to verify that it corresponds with Andy's public key, where v is the verification function:

v(message, public key, SIGNATURE)

The private key is Andy's own personal key for the transaction, while the public key is used by others to check it. The public key is the "send to" address, so when Andy sends Brenda 10 CRTC, he is really sending it to Brenda's public key. Note that these keys ARE IMBEDDED cryptographically within a string of characters that contain the messages and signature so it is impossible to figure them out.

A private key is generated by "key generation" programs. Some of these are resident in CRTC wallets (We will discuss wallets in more detail in Chapter 7).

An example of private key generated is:

2CF24DBA5FB0A30E26E83B2AC5B9E29E1B161E5C1FA7425E73043362

For example, in Bitcoin, a private wallet generator would look like the following:

1427L1ARMZ2AP2oHdUhwY9vuLCfGqfgX2u   10   CRTC
?15IJkaap9wkCnaUoXuwCxFLeXAtoW4C4

By a complicated mathematical algorithm behind the DIGITAL SIGNATURE, the nodes are able to check if Andy actually owned a private key, without actually seeing the private key because it is buried within the verification message. While the private key can be considered as the true password, the signature together with the private messages proves that Andy possesses the password without telling people what the private key is.

Because the math combines both the private key and a unique message, the password will be different for each transaction and cannot be used again by anyone else for another transaction. No one can also change the message as it passes through the network because any change in the message will nullify the signature, because the fraudulent or erroneous message will not agree with the thousands of other users who are processing the message. This is the Byzantine General problem solution in action!

The math behind creating the signature is really complex, and the signatures generated are comprised of numbers and letters that cannot be duplicated or tampered with because of the impossible levels of probability. For example, just for a private key, there can be 2 to the 256th possible combinations for a key. To drive this point home, 2 to the 40th power is

1,000,995,116,000. That is trillions; and to get to 2 to the 256th, multiply that number by and its products by two <u>216 more times</u>. The resulting number will nave close to 100 zeroes.

And what is the chances that Andy can send to a duplicate address or conversely, Brenda getting the same transaction from a duplicate address? Let us look at a mind boggling analogy as to the number of addresses. It is estimated that the total grains of sand on earth totals around 10,000,000,000,000,000,000. The total number of possible number CTRC addresses is equal to each of the 10,000,000,000,000,000,000 grains of sands having ANOTHER ENTIRE PLANET of the same number of grains of sand! If you ever figure out what that number is, it is still much smaller than the total number of total CTRC addresses.

<u>Assurance of transactions' accuracy and adequacy of funds</u>

We have seen how digital signatures work to make sure that each transaction is authorized and cannot be tampered with. But if Andy sends 10 CRTC to Brenda, how can the system be sure that Andy actually has the money to spend? Does Andy have money to pay? While a typical bank ledger would contain the balance of Andy's account if he had money in the bank, THERE ARE NO RECORDS OF ACCOUNT BALANCES at all in a cryptocurrency system.

Instead of balances, however, the ownership of CRTC is verified by different links to Andy's previous transactions.

To send the 10 CRTC to Brenda, Andy has to refer to previous transactions where he received at least 10 CRTC's. The CRTC system doesn't care how much money Andy has, it only cares whether he has 10 CRTC at the very moment that he transmits money to Brenda. These previous transactions referred to are called INPUTS. The other nodes in the CRTC network will verify these inputs to ensure that Andy was truly the recipient of money, and that these previous inputs total 10 or more CRTCs.

Let us see an example of this in action. The following ledger shows the INPUT data which tells us that Andy has more than enough of previous transactions to pay for the 10 CRTCs that he is sending to Brenda.

ANDY'S INPUT TRANSACTIONS

Previous Output	Amount	From address	Type	Script Sig
gh825usw1-1	1.1	sdfFJDfd4538J	Address	1e21f77tpiaebhsmk6ce
nw97u6ttb-a	2.4	m4BlKRpsQynA	Address	4rrw7gmz0dbispwjjwx5
4t89jmsoi-b	0.5	71fSZMoPGSS5	Address	q9ejzxo9y8v496dn43sh
Tsabkumaa-x	6.0	CQYbIbPiev8P	Address	papeqv7ld5z9n7dcenz3
k2dco5yoh-m	.8	mfEeEECC0A6S	Address	p5lghttvmadlyzaqp8pa

TOTAL: 11.3 (Enough to cover his transactions)

The CRTC system therefore, adds up the total INPUTS until it finds out that Andy has sufficient (at least 10 CRTC units) to pay Brenda.

The digital transactions that will be sent back to send 10 CRTCs to Brenda's account is called OUTPUT. Output actually, might have two components. One is sending the money to Brenda, and the other is sending change back to Andy just in case previous INPUTS exceed 10 CRTCs.

We can see that the ownership of CRTC is passed from one person to another via some kind of chain. Each transaction that that is processed is always dependent on previous transactions. To make sure that the nodes can trust the transactions that led to Andy's 10 CRTC's, the nodes' wallets will download all the transactions that were ever made and will check each of the transactions' validity from the VERY BEGINNING! It is very important for a wallet to validate these transactions especially since the CRTC system is populated by complete strangers.

<u>The Double Spending Issue – the time factor</u>

To summarize CRTC security, we can see that when the other system users verify the Digital Signature, only Andy could have created the transaction message "sending" money to Brenda. To make sure that Andy has enough funds to send Brenda, the users also check every past transaction referenced as input, to make sure that what Andy is sending Brenda is unspent.

There is still one hole that needs to be plugged in the CRTC system, and that is to prevent users like Andy from using the same money twice, by sending the same transaction one after another. If Andy only had 10 CRTC units to begin with, he could place two orders and receive both orders before the CRTC has time to check them:

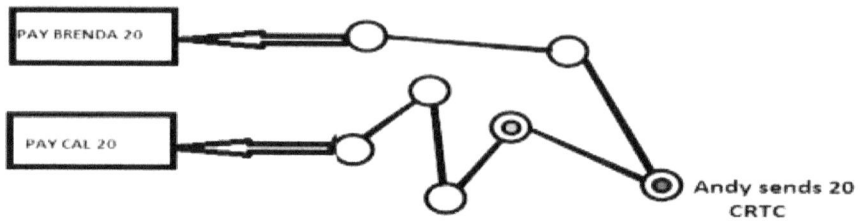

Because the transactions are passed along to each and every node in the CRTC system, the order in which they are received is the same as the order when they were created. Even so-called "timestamps" cannot be trusted because Andy could easily misrepresent the transaction time. Because there is no central computer to check the time, like a credit card or a bank system, there is no way to verify the correct chronological sequence.

Fraud is therefore possible because Andy can now wait for Brenda to ship her product, and then send another payment transaction to Cal, or even to himself using the same input references. If she is really unlucky, Brenda would have shipped the product and not get any money because Cal or even Andy would have gotten it first.

The solution to this is a "mathematical race" incorporated in the bedrock of a cryptocurrency system: The blockchain.

Chapter 5 - Blockchains and Mining – the Key to Cryptocurrency

<u>Definition</u>

A cryptocurrency system relies on a key component called a blockchain, and these two terms have sometimes been used interchangeably. The blockchain, which we will be describing in detail in this chapter, is the underlying protocol that allows for the transfer of cryptocurrency and ensures a bulletproof transaction verification system to avoid fraud and malice. It is the most significant and powerful development in cryptocurrency technology. The power of this technology also lies in its capability in distributing information across all the individual computers (called nodes) within the system. The term blockchain has often been interchanged with distributed ledger technology.

The advantage of blockchain is it is distributed across all the nodes in the system. A particular cryptocurrency's blockchain database does not exist in a single location or is under the control of a single central authority, but exists or is hosted by thousands of computers at any single time.

The blockchain network contains a self-review or auditing system that because of the thousands of users confirming transactions, practically guarantee the accuracy and integrity of transactions and data residing in its ledgers. This security feature of a blockchain system is mostly brought about by the cryptographic manipulation and verification of data making it mathematically improbable to manipulate, change, and duplicate transactions. Not even massive computer power can hope to disrupt the blockchain system.

Blockchains are composed of three core parts:

<u>The Block:</u> This is simply transactions that are listed in a ledger over time. The amount, the time period, the number of transactions, and the even that triggered the creation of the block (payment, transfer, receipt) is different for each block. It would look like the following, non-digitally:

```
BLOCK ANDY
Transaction 1
Transaction 2
Transaction 3
Transactoin 4
```

Chain: Every block contains a hash of the previous block that "chained" it to the previous one. A computed hash successfully computed by a node mathematically links the block to another block. This concept is one of the most complex and difficult ones to understand in the cryptocurrency system, because it requires the use of fairly advanced arithmetic. But the chain is the glue magic that links the blocks together and provides the system of mathematical "trust" where no other trust exists in the cryptographic universe.

Hash: A very unique mathematical "signature" that is created from the information in a preceding block. Consider the hash as a unique fingerprint that solidly locks in the blocks together in time and order. Cryptograhic hashing which creates the hash, was invented many decades ago, and was incorporated into cryptocurrency systems to provide unique identifiers for their transactions. This was the only "out" that the founders of cryptocurrency system saw that could replace the trust function of traditional currency and monetary systems.

Hashing generates a one-way mechanism which cannot be decrypted by creating a mathematical algorithm that orders data of a specified size and reducing it to a string of bits with a fixed size. The typical bit is about thirty two characters long. This string is a numerical representation of the data in the blockchain that was just "hashed" or encrypted.

A quick note on the math used in cryptocurrencies: Bitcoin uses the Secure Hash Algorithm (SHA) as a cryptographic hash functions used in its blockchains. It is a one of the most widely known algorithms and creates a unique, fixed-size 256-bit (32-byte) fixed-size hash.

<u>Network</u>: The network is comprised of "full nodes." Together they function as a single mechanism running an algorithm that secures the network. Each node will have a complete record of all the transactions that were ever recorded in that blockchain.

The advantage of blockchain is it is distributed across all the nodes in the system. A particular cryptocurrency's blockchain database does not exist in a single location or is under the control of a single central authority, but exists or is hosted by thousands of computers at any single time.

The blockchain network contains a self-review or auditing system that because of the thousands of users confirming transactions, practically guarantee the accuracy and integrity of transactions and data residing in its ledgers. This security feature of a blockchain system is mostly brought about by the cryptographic manipulation and verification of data making it mathematically improbable to manipulate, change, and duplicate transactions. Not even massive computer power can hope to disrupt the blockchain system.

<u>Proper ordering</u>

To start the blockchain process, Andy's transaction is placed in correct order by including his transaction in a block together with a group of other transactions. It then eventually links them in the block chain after the fulfillment of a set of conditions.

Do not confuse this with the transactions to determine if Andy had enough CRTC to be able to pay Brenda. Those transactions tracked how Andy accumulated ownership of CRTC, while the block chain is used to put transactions in order:

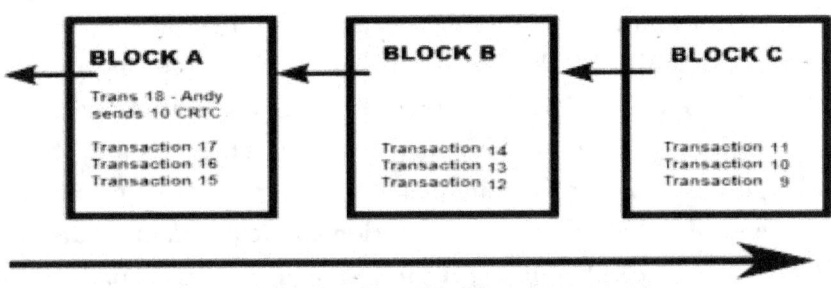

Note from the above diagram that every block references the past immediate block, placing the blocks in chronological order. It is possible to go back all the way back in time to reference the very first block of transactions ever made. Transactions in Block A, where Andy's transaction is, happened at the same time, while transactions not yet grouped in a block are "unconfirmed" or "unordered":

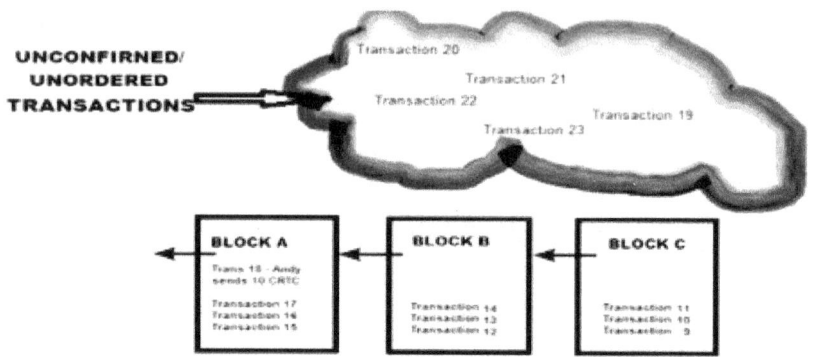

Any user can accumulate a set of unordered transactions and assemble them in a block. This new block is then broadcast to the rest of the system, suggesting that it should be the next block in the chain. With thousands of users or nodes in the system, several of them can create new blocks simultaneously. These blocks need to be ordered somehow, and not in the order of when they arrive, because new blocks can appear at the same time in different points in the system. How does the network accomplish this ordering?

Mathematical puzzles and miners

The solution is that a contest now ensues where a valid block should contain the solution to a complex mathematical problem. The nodes' computers run the entire block text of through random guessing programs called a CRYPTOGRAPHIC HASH until it arrives at at the correct answer. We will not go into the mathematical detail of the "hashing" because of the lengthy explanation that might appeal to a mathematics oriented few.

All we need to know is that the solution to the problem is totally unpredictable, and the only way to get the correct answer is through random guesses. Because of the hashing requirements and the extremely high number of possibilities, it takes several years of manual guessing to get to the right answer. In the cryptocurrency system, since there are thousands of computers working 24/7, it takes an average of about 10 minutes for a correct solution to come up, meaning that a new block is "chained" to the block chain every ten minutes.

The first node or person to solve the problem will then broadcast their "winning" block and this block of transactions is now accepted as the next block in the chain. The extreme randomness in the complex problem makes it unlikely for two or more people to arrive at the solution at the same time. Unlikely however, does not mean never, and occasionally two blocks will be solved at the same time. The system will have a "tie-breaker" system that involves the ultimate winning node to have solved another problem and determining who the winner is by how much transactions they have in their blocks.

The block is finally created after tremendous work using powerful computers engaging in what is essentially a shoot and miss trial-and-error computational exercise. A "miner" will finally emerge with the one block hash containing the cryptocurrency algorithm was waiting and looking for – a mathematical answer with the exact number of zeros required together with various other conditions.

The mathematical puzzles are so complex and difficult, that users are sure that it is impossible for an "attacker" to come in and insert bogus answers to the blockchain problems. Nodes trust the cryptocurrency protocol to protect users from such invaders, but no trust is required among the users.

With tens of thousands of miners working continuously, we have seen that nothing in the processes that we have described requires trust between the people working the problems. If anything, miners want other miners to fail in their cryptographic work so that they can get to add a new block to the chain first, and collect their cryptocurrency payment.

Chapter 6 - Putting It All Together – Mining, Buying And Selling With Cryptocurrency

With knowledge of the inner workings of blockchain technology, we will now turn to how people acquire, sell, and enter into various cryptocurrencies and how they are used in real-world commerce.

The granddaddy of cryptocurrency, Bitcoin has often been mentioned interchangeably with cryptocurrency itself. As of July 31, 2017, there were about 16 million Bitcoin in circulation with a market value of almost 70 billion U.S. dollars. The "top 100" cryptocurrencies have a market value of over 150 billion USD. This amount of purchasing power is pretty substantial and cryptocurrencies are being used with increasing frequency and regularity as more people continue to (1) know about them, (2) appreciate their qualities, and (3) understand how their limitations.

The "mining" reward

When we discussed blockchains in the previous chapter, we saw that they are "completed" by users who are willing to solve mathematical puzzles. After proof of work is established, the first node to get the answer to the math problem broadcasts the "successful" block, which is now accepted as the next block to be linked in the chain. The high number of people trying to solve the puzzles together with the extreme randomness of the math problem makes it practically impossible for two or more people to come up with the correct answer at the same time. In mining, the more hashes are completed, the higher the chances a block can be linked to the block chain, together with the chances of earning cryptocurrency increases.

Nodes are solving for, and computing the cryptographic puzzles all over the world, and anyone with a computer can simply take their shot at it. It can become costly, difficult, and with more and more people trying to solve the cryptographic puzzles every day, more time-consuming and requiring increasing amounts of computer power. Unless someone is just trying to have fun solving complex algorithms, they do it with a reward in mind. Those who do this dirty digital digging are called "miners".

The cryptocurrency ecosystem incentivizes miners by rewarding them with tokens and cryptocurrency units every time they solve a blockchain.

The cryptocurrency algorithm rewards them for essentially providing a service for all users of the network. This effort is done either individually or by mining pools.

Mining for cryptocurrency

If you are really up to the investment of time and money, you need to purchase the requisite hardware and software for the effort. In the "good old days" (really just about five years ago), you could get by with just an above average CPU to do the hash work and the cryptography required to complete block chains. Specialized hardware and accessories in the market today are available from $5,000 USD and up.

You also need to have the proper software to help you mine cryptocurrency. Many of these can be downloaded for free, while some products will require either a purchase or subscription for their supposed "extra features" to help you along. Cryptocurrency mining software are supposed to do the highly complex perform complex hash calculations, towards solving the mathematical puzzles.

Many people have entered into cryptocurrency mining full-time, and the effort not only includes putting money, but also keeping up to date with the latest news and developments. With computer technology moving forward at the rate that it is, serious miners cannot afford to be left behind.

Mining pools

"Solo mining" is either too time consuming and/or expensive for some people. Instead, they join mining pools to help increase their chances of getting cryptocurrency. Special equipment and software is used whether cryptocurrency is mined individually or in pools. In mining pools, members get shares of cryptocurrency earned for "successful" hashes.

While the share an individual gets from a successfully linked block chain (or solved puzzle) is smaller than if an individual mined it, the chances of success are increased when more people work on the blocks.

Getting and earning cryptocurrency the "easy" way

If you don't want to spend the time, money, and computing power to mine for bitcoin, a much easier way to get or earn cryptocurrency is to sell goods and services and tell people that you are using cryptocurrency. Most vendors who accept cryptocurrency seem to take only Bitcoin, but a growing number of cryptocurrency are gaining the necessary reputation to gain wider acceptance.

A good first step to earning cryptocurrency is to sell merchandise on Ebay or be a registered vendor in online marketplaces that accept bitcoin for payment. These are forward looking business enterprises payment systems have been configured to allow for the receipt of Bitcoin for payment. On Ebay for example, Paypal is now equipped to take Bitcoin deposits to be used as payment.

<u>Buying with cryptocurrency</u>

A growing list of companies in the United States, as well as online stores abroad take cryptocurrency especially Bitcoin, as payment. Among the well-known places that accept Bitcoin include: Overstock.com, Microsoft, Subway, Virgin Galactic, travel booking sites Expedia and CheapAir.com, and the gaming portal Zynga. You can also purchase from Gap, GameStop and JC Penney if you use eGifter.com.

Regardless of how you obtain, earn, or spend cryptocurrency, you will need a digital/electronic "wallet" to keep your money in.

Chapter 7 - Getting Cryptocurrencies – Wallets and Exchanges
<u>Cryptocurrency digital wallets</u>

For most people, block chain, hashes, and cryptographic algorithms are a bit too much to deal with for those who just want to accumulate cryptocurrencies or use it as currency. No matter how you obtain or use cryptocurrency, you need a digital wallet to house the cryptocurrency in.

You need the wallet to store, receive, and send cryptocurrency unless you have developed a sophisticated method to warehouse it. Most of the coins in circulation such as Bitcoin, Ethereum, and Litecoin actually have "official" wallets, or they recommend third party ones that conform to their particular cryptocurrency.

Unlike typical physical wallets, digital wallets do not actually contain or store cryptocurrency. In Chapter 3, we discussed how cryptocurrency systems are all about maintaining transaction ledgers and simply add and subtract the amounts of your total cryptocurrency transactions and determine how much your "balance" is. In fact, the most important "item" stored in a digital wallet is the private and public keys that we discussed earlier. A reputable wallet will store a personal ledger of transactions involving your personal accounts.

The digital wallet will allow anyone to perform electronic transactions which includes online purchases and sales. A digital wallet also allows an owner to link a bank account with the wallet. This can be useful if there is a desire to purchase or sell cryptocurrency and using regular dollars to purchase or sell them. Some wallets even allow for the storage of identification cards like insurance or health cards, drivers licenses, membership cards, loyalty cards and others. These credentials can then be transmitted wirelessly to a merchant terminal by using Near Field Communication, or NFC technology. In NFC, the phone is simply placed again a reader to complete a transaction.

In effect, digital wallets not only allow purchase and sale transactions but also related authentication processes to validated personal credentials. For example, the digital wallet can be used to validate someone using cryptocurrency to buy alcohol with the wallet owner's credentials that contain his age.

The best feature of the wallet is that the validation work that is conducted by the system to verify transactions, hashes, addresses, etc. are done in the background and is simply picked up by the wallet as transactions to be read and included in your history.

There are hundreds of digital wallet platforms available today, and the more prominent ones, like Coinbase and Mycelium are all free to join, have good reputations, and are pretty easy to sign up for. After using Google Play or the Itunes store to install the wallet app, the user only needs to enter very little pertinent information. Aside from an e-mail address, no other personal information is required. Sales and purchases are practically single click transactions. If the user has previous bitcoin transactions, these will be located when the system locates the private key that the user has been using.

<u>Wallet security</u>

While cryptocurrency wallets are designed to be secure and generally anonymous, security actually varies from one wallet to another. Ultimately, just a regular physical wallet or any other (non-cryptocurrency) digital wallet, the safety and security will depend on common sense practices. Many serious users maintain more than one wallet, using each separate wallet for different reasons. Added security layers include the encryption of the wallet, the use of something like a Google authenticator, or the use of multi-signature transactions.

It is also a good idea to back up the "contents" of a wallet, especially the private keys. Contents can be used typical backup systems like a thumb drive or portable hard drive. As to privacy and anonymity, the obvious answer is you should not put any specific identifying marks on your wallet via your private key or your login name. The cryptocurrency ecosystem is public and open source in nature with the blockchain ledgers being subject to scrutiny by everyone. It is possible to reverse engineer information to identify someone specifically, but it would be an extremely difficult process. If you are smart and try to leave as inconspicuous a footprint as possible, it is almost a lock that you will be anonymous during your existence in the cryptocurrency universe.

Which wallet?

There are many "brands" of digital wallets in the cryptocurrency ecosystem that advertise their own supposedly wonderful features and advantages. But no matter what that brand is, All wallets should be able to allow a user to access their information on a hand held gadget, desktop, or laptop. The following are the types of wallets available:

Mobile – Run from an app that can be used on your smartphone or tablet.

Desktop – Run from a desktop application that is connected to a cryptocurrency system directly. Desktops and mobile devices are the most common forms of a digital wallet.

Hardware – These are devices that are dedicated to "hold" cryptocurrency transaction information and keep it secure. This can be in the form of USB devices for example and can connect online to access the cryptocurrency system.

Online - This wallet is essentially web-based, where the information is available on a server.

Paper - A QR code is printed for the private and public keys. This option allows someone to not store any digital data or leave any form of identity online.

A word of caution: Regardless of the form you choose as your cryptocurrency wallet, if you lose or misplace your private key, you will lose your "money". If you lose your cryptocurrency because you lost your key, you are out of luck.

Cryptocurrency exchanges

Parties interested in publicly trading in stocks have the New York Stock Exchange and NASDAQ, and those who want to publicly buy and sell practically everything else has the Chicago Mercantile Exchange. These exchanges locate and link together buyers and sellers of financial instruments (including currency), and post current market prices to guide the parties interested in trading. There are no such mega exchanges that deal with cryptocurrency as of the present.

While no such facility yet exists for cryptocurrency, there are many public exchanges on websites where people can buy, sell, trade, and even exchange cryptocurrencies not only for conventional fiat currency like U.S.

dollars and the Euro, but also for other cryptocurrency issues. Someone wanting to trade in Bitcoin using Litecoin can google "cryptocurrency exchanges" to see what outfits are engaged in public trading.

These exchanges are all private businesses and are not generally subject to any regulatory oversight by any country's government. A lot of them are also based outside the United States, so extreme care must be taken before considering them. Some exchanges offer themselves to more "advanced" traders, by allowing for the execution of highly specialized and esoteric transactions like liquidity swaps. They may also allow for short-selling and margin trading. It is important to note that most of them have been around for less than ten years, so their stability and reputation are not yet quite tested.

People can use some exchanges on a one-time basis, without having to provide too much information to register, such as providing addresses and social security numbers. Others who want to trade full-time and "professionally" will likely need to provide multiple identification and will be required to open an account.

There are three basic kinds of cryptocurrency exchanges:

Direct Trades – In these platforms, people meet directly with other parties from other countries to exchange currencies. The parties agree on a price or exchange rate.

Trade Platforms – Buyers and sellers are connected through what is essentially a website "meeting place". The website owner where the trading parties connect take a fee from each transaction.

Brokerages - These are websites where any interested party can by cryptocurrencies at prices set at the brokerage. These function essentially as money changers in the real currency markets.

As in anything else that requires an outlay of money, some preparatory work should be done before joining an exchange, much less part with hard-earned money. The following are what prospective investors and traders should consider:

Reputation – Unlike exchanges of traditional financial and commercial products, cryptocurrency exchanges have not been around for a very long time. The ideal way to find out about the integrity of an exchange is through third party testimonies and personal experiences of others. With the explosion of cryptocurrency, there are many online discussion forums where exchanges are discussed and even rated.

Fees and charges - A reputable exchange will disclose what their fees are up front. A prospective customer should know what charges and fees are for different transactions, such as transfers, payments, and even receipts. It pays to compare fees not only as absolute amounts, but also consider the quality, speed, and transparency of the services rendered.

Funding and payment - It is important that an exchange offers multiple ways to allow someone to transfer funds in and out of an exchange. There are a variety of ways that money can flow in and out: Debit cards, direct debits of bank accounts, wire transfers, PayPal, and even credit cards. Wire transfers usually require a lot of documentation up front, while credit card transactions will usually demand sufficient identification before a transaction is approved. Privacy and security can be compromised if the exchange has limited funding options.

Most trading platforms in the United States and the U.K. will ask for government-issued I.D. before they allow withdrawals and deposits. Some of these verification procedures can take days, but they exist to protect everyone from problems in dealing with what is essentially an unregulated financial instrument. There are other exchanges outside those countries' jurisdictions however, that will allow traders to keep their anonymity.

Some foreign exchanges may have restrictions if transactions are done of the United States or other Western European countries. Other countries' looser regulatory structures may run afoul of reporting requirements in the U.S. It is important to consider what functions and tools are allowable and legal across international borders.

Exchange rates – When using an exchange domiciled in other countries, exchanging cryptocurrency for U.S. dollars may require not only a fee, but also a steep foreign exchange conversion difference. Rate fluctuations and fees can sometimes be up to 10% of the total transaction value. Once again it pays to shop around for more favorable foreign exchange policies.

Chapter 8 - The Future of Cryptocurrency

You can walk into Helen's Pizza store in Bergen New Jersey without any cash, credit, or debit card and still fill yourself up with a pepperoni slice and a soda. To pay for your meal, you point your phone at a sign beside the cash register and in an instant, you have paid for your meal using cryptocurrency, in this case, Bitcoin. If pizza is not your thing, you can walk a few blocks and get a sub at a Subway location and pay digitally as well.

You can also pay using cryptocurrency for travel (Expedia and Virgin), merchandise (Overstock.com), and for software from Microsoft. Microsoft founder Bill Gates is a supporter of cryptocurrency and thinks that it is a electronic revolution of tsunami proportions that cannot be avoided, but needs to be embraced and accepted.

The popularity of cryptocurrency has increased on a logarithmic scale ever since it became a public medium of exchange less than ten years ago. The very first Bitcoin released in 2009 had a value of less than a penny with just a few thousand being issued by the founders. Not a single commercial transaction occurred using Bitcoin until 201o. One of the first transactions, which became widely famous was the issuance of 10,000 Bitcoin units to purchase $25 worth of pizza.

This means that at the time, Bitcoin was valued at only $.0025 per unit. By the middle of 2017, the average monthly Bitcoin volume was over $60 billion dollars representing almost 2,000,000 transactions. Probably the most astounding statistic that a Bitcoin unit as of the end of July, 2017 is valued at around $4,000. This means that if you bought $10.00 worth of Bitcoin in 2009, that "portfolio" would be worth $50 million today!

But outside of Bitcoin, the cryptocurrency market is also exploding. With over seven hundred systems available, paying using this new digital currency is becoming more widespread. The scale of the use of currency is either alarming or promising, depending on one's viewpoint.

And while cryptocurrency is not yet traded on any major commodity exchange, the New York Stock Exchange in 2015 began posting bitcoin price index with the symbol NYXBT, a major acknowledgement not only of the existence of cryptocurrency, but also of its growing notoriety and use. The NYXBT price is posted every afternoon and also published at the exchange's Global Index Feed, or GIF. Cryptocurrency has grown way beyond being anonymous and staying under the radar, and both its currency value and use are growing.

Total cryptocurrency in circulation is just below 9% of total U.S. dollar currency in circulation. This means that almost 1 out of 10 transaction dollars is made in cryptocurrency. Bitcoin are mostly used in transactions using smart phones, and with a big percentage of people now doing their commerce on portable gadgets, cryptocurrency's share of total business transactions is expected to increase. To what extent this will happen largely depends on how reliable in continues to be in providing anonymity and rock solid mathematical soundness.

Through July 31, 2017, cryptocurrency use is legal in most countries, which means that currencies such as Bitcoin can be used to buy or sell goods and services. There are very few countries where cryptocurrency is illegal. What clouds the legality issue is that a unit of cryptocurrency itself cannot be bought or sold in some countries. As more people in the less "stable" nations begin to appreciate and know about cryptocurrency, they can begin comparing it to their own sovereign currencies and may conclude that stability-wise, what their central banks circulate is not as attractive as cryptocurrency.

There are financial executives in the United States who are also trying to incorporate cryptocurrencies in other financial instruments such as derivatives and exchange traded funds. While there are the expected bumps in the road with the Securities and Exchange Commission and other agencies, the momentum to move cryptocurrency beyond its current reputation as an underground currency for nerds seems to be building.

With blockchain technology being considered in other applications, its growing reputation can only add to the viability and reliability of cryptocurrency. For example, there is a growing interest in "smart contracts," where computer protocols can execute and complete the provisions of a contract without requiring a trusted third party to verify and validate them.

The growing interest towards block chain applications has put the spotlight on cryptocurrency, because it is the first ostensibly successful application of the technology applied universally. The gatekeepers of the cryptocurrency world will be best served to make sure their ecosystem survives and thrives.

Conclusion

Cryptocurrency is not the next big investment technology, It has already arrived!.. It needs to be accepted and respected as a new way of doing business, and one that is done by not just regular people, but by a class of people considered smarter than the rest of the general population. User profiles suggest that a majority of cryptocurrency users are highly educated and computer literate.

For all its promises, however, there some serious concerns about their use and their long-term viability.

Because of its anonymity, many people tend to use it for nefarious purposes. On the dark web, you can purchase illegal goods and services with Bitcoin and other cryptocurrencies. There have been some highly publicized arrests over the use of some of the purchases, and while the perpetrators and the dark web were the focus, cryptocurrency was the secondary character in the legal and law enforcement scenarios that unfolded. The danger with bad press is not just that cryptocurrency may lose its appeal and value with regular users. A bigger danger to cryptocurrency viability is that that sovereign governments may decide to shut down a cryptocurrency system if its use violates national interests.

The other issue that will be interesting to watch will be how the system protocol for Bitcoin will adjust to "compensate" miners when Bitcoin issuance ceases in 2041. Miners get "paid" by being awarded Bitcoin for linking blockchains. Because miners verify and validate transactions, they are essential to the survival and operation to the cryptocurrency system. Since they will no longer be able to mine for bitcoins, will the system protocol instead pay them a fee? If so, in what form will this compensation take?

A much talked (complained?) about downside in cryptocurrency systems is the lack of fallback or insurance in case you lose your private key, or if somehow your cryptocurrency disappears into thin air. More than anything else, this is what keeps a big number of people from even thinking of jumping into the cryptocurrency waters. With a Bitcoin unit trading near $5,000, it is a big commitment to trust something that has no physical presence, with no guarantee against loss due to negligence or fraud. As this "no central authority" trust system is central to the cryptocurrency model, insurance and a 1-800 customer support number is not likely to be available.

Computer power requirements also represents another potential risk and disadvantage of the cryptocurrency system. In the unlikely event that a catastrophic event wipes out power and electricity over an extended period of time, commercial activity around a cryptocurrency will come to a halt. People will not have any physical currency to pull out of their pockets to pay for goods and services. Whatever purchasing power or monetary assets in a cryptocurrency system are essentially useless and non-existent in a world without adequate computing power and worse, with no computing power at all.

Ultimately however, we are in the digital age and cryptocurrency by definition, is digital currency. If we are to keep up with the times, our financial systems need to keep up with the digitization of the rest of our lives.

Cryptocurrency is quickly emerging from the depths of algorithmic mystery as just some form of shadow currency. While you may not yet buy your first unit of cryptocurrency after reading my book, I trust that you now know more than you need than just a surface grasp of its concepts.

I hope this book is able to help you to get a working knowledge of cryptocurrencies and their underlying systems and trust that you are now ready to apply everything you have learned from this book (if you have not done so already)

Ethereum
Learn Fast!
What you need to know to make money in an hour

Introduction

Ethereum is a platform that runs on a network of nodes (computers), which make certain that information and special computer applications known as smart contracts are duplicated and processed – even with the absence of a centralized server. If you haven't understood a thing of what you have just read, don't worry. You will later learn more about Ethereum and how you can make money out of it.

Ethereum is a project that was supported through a crowdfunding effort in 2014, and it is now being developed by the Ethereum Foundation - a non-profit organization based in Switzerland.

In this book, you will learn the skills you need to make sure that investing in Ethereum through holding or trading Ether tokens will be worthwhile. Specifically, you will get to know:

- How Ethereum works and how it is different compared to the blockchain technology used in Bitcoin

- The process of Ethereum mining and how you can consider it as another option to make money in cryptocurrency

- How investors are taking hold of Ether tokens to make substantial revenue in the possible upsurge of the token's value

- Other digital currencies that show potential value aside from Bitcoin and Ether

- The future prospects of Ethereum and the current hurdles that should be resolved by the platform

Chapter 1 –What is Ethereum?

It will be easier to understand the nature of Ethereum if you have background knowledge on how the Internet works.

At present, our personal profile, financial information, and passwords are mostly stored in servers and data storage controlled by big players like Google, Facebook, and Amazon. Even the articles and blogs you are reading online are stored on a cloud owned by an organization that requires fees for keeping all the data.

This arrangement has numerous advantages as these organizations employ teams of data professionals to assist in keeping and securing information and help in eliminating the costs that usually come with hosting and uptime.

But there are also loopholes with these advantages. Cyber criminals, even government agencies, can have access to your data without your permission, by hacking or controlling a third-party service. Your personal information could be leaked or even modified.

The founder of Apache Web Server, Brian Behlendorf has gone so far as calling this centralized setup the "original sin" of the Internet. Advocates like him insist that the Internet should be decentralized. They highlight the risks of having a centralized design of the World Wide Web. Well, a movement has emerged around utilizing new tools such as the blockchain technology, to help attain this objective.

One of the recent technologies that take part in this splintered movement is Ethereum. Unlike Bitcoin, which aims to replace online banking, the main objective of Ethereum is to use blockchain to disrupt online third-party services.

The Global Computer

Ethereum's goal is to be a "global computer" that would not stick to the centralized user-server setup. There are also people who argue that Ethereum will democratize the current system.

With Ethereum, nodes will replace the conventional clouds and servers. These communication points are controlled by groups of volunteers located around the world.

The objective is that Ethereum would perform the same functionality to users anywhere across the globe, allowing people to compete in providing services on top of this infrastructure.

Browsing through an application store, for instance, you will find different types of applications that can be used in every aspect of life. These applications depend on a third-party service to keep your financial information, transaction data, and other personal information in their respective clouds or servers.

If everything works according to the vision, Ethereum will allow the owner of these applications to take control of the data as well as have creative rights. The point is that third parties can no longer have access to your data, and that one entity can no longer curate or censor your applications. Again, only the owner can input changes, not any entity.

In the proposed theory, it integrates the control that users had over their data in the past with accessible insights that we're used to in the digital era. Every time you input or delete notes, every communication point on the web makes the change.

Somehow the concept has been mixed with skepticism.

Even though the applications don't seem impossible, it's uncertain which apps will actually be helpful, secure, or can be quantified – and if they will be as efficient to use as the applications we have today.

With blockchain technology, Ethereum became an open source tool that gives developers authority to create over a decentralized app. With its highest hash rate value, which is 3 TeraHash, it has a huge infrastructure. Vitalik Buterin with the help of his co-developers, Charles Hoskinson, Mihai Alisie, and Anthony Di Lorio, created Ethereum for high-grade graphics processing units.

Because Ethereum is working on blockchain networks, it also comes with the conveniences of decentralized networks such as:

- Inability of other entities to input changes on data.

- Prevention of fraudulent activities caused by cyber criminals or hackers.

- Zero percent chance of applications to be turned off or crash.

The distribution of Ethereum was made possible through a public blockchain network, which is in the form of Initial Coin Offering (ICO). In ICO, more or less 35,000 Bitcoins were traded for about 60 million. This allowed an estimated amount of $ 14 million to be raised, which comprised 14% of stocks.

Moreover, the distribution of Ethereum continues to work through an ICO, in which it works at the same time with the distribution of Ether. ETH or Ether is known as the Ethereum platform's cryptocurrency token.

In Ethereum, a blockchain introduces blocks of various scalability. At the same time, there are different kinds of user accounts that raise with 22 byte addresses. There are two kinds of accounts – the external account which is the account with private keys, and the other one is the contract account which is the account with contract codes.

The authority that controls them is one of the major distinctions between the external and contract accounts.

Contract accounts are controlled by internal codes. While they can utilize contract accounts, people need external accounts to enable contract accounts. Moreover, contract accounts are permitted to execute transactions if ordered by external accounts.

Therefore, unless triggered by external accounts, these contract accounts cannot execute their usual operations such as Random Number Generation and API calls. On the other side, the control for external accounts is handed to human users since these users can control private keys, which consequently return control to external accounts.

Smart Contracts

Smart Contracts (or the use of scripting functionality) is one of the most significant features of Ethereum platform. This allows users to produce tokens that are suitable with wallets and exchanges under a standard coin API (application programming interface).

Moreover, this shows that it can speed up the exchange of money, stocks, or property. And thereby, with the use of smart contracts, we can count on a self-operating program that facilitates orders immediately once conditions are approved. Since their works are executed through a blockchain network, they operate according to how it was programmed. They execute without the possibility of being interfered by other entities, and without the chance of censorship or downtime.

Here's an overview of a smart contract's operations:

- Initially, a code from an option contract is given into the blockchain network. Although the contract serves as the public ledger, this code is given with the security from the concealment of both parties.

- A smart contract is completed once a period expires and strike prices has been reached.

- Finally, since a smart contract was executed, regulators will start monitoring the activities of the market by utilizing the blockchain network. Nevertheless, all throughout the monitoring, regulators are required to secure the privacy of both parties.

Chapter 2 - How Ethereum Works

In terms of structure, the Ethereum blockchain is quite similar to that of Bitcoin. Both have the capacity to record the whole transaction history, and each node in the network can keep a copy of the transactions.

The main difference with the Ethereum network is that the nodes are stored in the most recent state of every smart contract on top of all Ether transactions. The platform has to monitor the status of the current data for all the applications, which includes the balance of the user, the smart contract codes, and the storage location.

When it comes to Bitcoin, the platform is using unspent transaction outputs to monitor who has how much digital currency. Even though it may seem complicated, the concept is actually quite easy to understand. Each time there is a Bitcoin transaction, the network will break the total amount as if it is fiat money issuing back Bitcoins in a manner that will make the information behave similarly to actual change.

In making future transactions, the Bitcoin platform should add up all your changes that are categorized as either unspent or spent. On the other hand, the Ethereum network uses accounts.

Similar to bank accounts, Ether tokens will appear in a digital wallet, and could be transferred into another account. The funds can be easily accessed, although the concept of continued relationship is non-existent.

The Ethereum Virtual Machine

In the Ethereum platform, each time an application is used, the network of thousands of computers will take charge of the processing. The contracts that are written in a specified smart contract programming language are compiled into the bytecode, which features the Ethereum Virtual Machine (EVM) that has the ability to execute and read.

All Ethereum nodes execute the contract using EVMs. Take note that each node in the network holds a duplicate of the transaction and smart contract record of the platform aside from monitoring the present state. Each time a user performs an action, the network nodes will agree that change has occurred.

The objective here is for the network of nodes and miners to take charge of the transfer instead of relying on third-party accounts such as banks or Pay-

Pal. Bitcoin miners will confirm the transfer of ownership of Bitcoin from one party to another, and the EVM will execute the contract with any rules that the developer will program in the onset.

Actual calculation on the EVM can be achieved via a machine readable language. However, developers could write smart contracts in high-level languages (such as Serpent and Solidify) that are easier for people to understand.

Smart Contracts

As with most concepts in the blockchain sector, most people are also confused over smart contracts, which is an emerging technology made possible through public blockchains. It can be difficult to understand mainly because the term doesn't clearly describe the core interaction.

Even though a basic contract will define the parameters of the relationship (typically legally binding), a smart contract will enforce a relationship with cryptographic code. Smart contracts are designed with special programs that specifically execute as defined.

First developed in 1993, the concept was originally explored by Nick Szabo – a cryptographer and computer scientist. He viewed smart contracts as some sort of digital vending machine. He described how users can input value or data and the machine will deliver a specified item.

Ethereum users could send one Ether token to anyone in the network anytime through a smart contract. In this example, the user will create an agreement, defining the specifics of the data to the contract so that it can execute specific commands.

Basically, Ethereum serves as a platform that is specifically designed for establishing smart contracts.

However, these new tools are not designed to be used as standalone as they can also compose the essential elements of decentralized applications (dApps) and even entire decentralized autonomous organizations (DAOs).

It is interesting to note that the Bitcoin network was the first platform to support basic smart contracts in the sense that the network could transmit value from one party to another. The node network could only validate transactions if specific conditions are met. However, Bitcoin is quite limited in the currency use case.

In contrast, Ethereum replaces the more restrictive design of Bitcoin and instead uses a programming language, which enables anyone with the right skillset to write their own applications. The network enables developers to program their own smart contracts or also known as autonomous agents. The programming language is regarded as a Turing complete, which means it can support a wider range of instructions and calculations.

Smart contracts can also serve as accounts for multi-signature so that the funds will only be spent if consensus has been reached. It can also take care of agreements between users and store details relevant to the app like membership records or domain registration.

Furthermore, smart contracts are likely to require assistance from other individual smart contracts. If someone will place a standard bet to project the temperature during a summer day, it could trigger a series of contracts under the hood. A contract will use external data to figure out the weather, and another contract will settle the bet according to the information it has received from the first contract once the conditions are met.

Running every contract will require transaction costs in form of Ether tokens that is largely based on the level of computational capacity required. The platform will execute the smart contracts using bytecode or a sequence of 1s and 0s, which could be read by the platform.

Chapter 3 – The Technology behind Ethereum

The Ethereum network allows developers to build and use decentralized applications (dApps) that serve specific purposes to its users. For example, Bitcoin is a form of dApp that provides users with a peer-to-peer electronic cash system that allows online Bitcoin payments. DApps are composed of code that are running on a blockchain network and not controlled by any central entity or individual.

With Ethereum, any centralized services could be decentralized. Consider all intermediary services, which exist across different industries – from conventional services (such as loans offered by financial institutions) to intermediary services (like regulatory compliance, voting systems, and title registries).

The Ethereum network can also be used in building decentralized autonomous organizations (DAOs), which are completely independent and have no centralized authority. These are operated by programming code, on a collection of smart contracts integrated in the Ethereum blockchain. The code is programmed to alter the structure and rules of a conventional organization to get rid of the need for centralized regulation. A DAO is owned by everyone who buy tokens, but tokens are equal to ownership and equity shares. The tokens serve as a symbol of contribution that grants people with voting rights.

Ethereum Decentralized Platform - The Pros

Since dApps are running using blockchain technology, they can also take advantage of its beneficial properties. This includes:

- Zero downtime – applications never go down and could never be switched off.

- Security – With no centralized point of failure and improved security through cryptography, decentralized applications are well protected against fraudulent activities and hack attempts.

- Tamper and corruption proof – Applications are based on a network that is built around the concept of consensus, making censorship impossible.

- Immutability – no third party can alter the data in the application

Ethereum Decentralized Platform - The Cons

Even though Ethereum offers numerous advantages, it's not 100% fool-proof. Remember, the code for smart contracts is written by humans, so they are only as good as the programmers. Oversights or code bugs could lead to unintended adverse effects. If a bug in the code is taken advantage, there is no surefire way of preventing the attack other than getting a network consensus and then reprogramming the root code. This is against the core concept of blockchain, given that it's designed to be immutable. In addition, any action that is taken by a centralized party could raise serious questions about the decentralized nature of an application.

Developing a Decentralized Application in the Ethereum Network

There are several ways that you could plug into the Ethereum platform. Among the easiest ways is using the native Mist browser that provides a basic interface and online wallet for storing and trading Ether and to create, manage, and store smart contracts. Similar to browsers that provide access and help people to browse the internet, Mist offers a portal into the world of dApps.

Another extension is MetaMask, which converts Google Chrome into the Ethereum platform. MetaMask enables anyone to easily develop and run dApps from their browser. While it is originally designed as a Chrome plugin, MetaMask will gradually be available for Firefox and a range of other web browsers.

Although these are still on beta version, MetaMask, Mist, and other browsers are set to make blockchain applications more accessible in the coming years. Even users without technical background could easily build blockchain applications, which is a significant development for blockchain technology and could raise dApps into mainstream use.

Current Applications Being Developed in the Ethereum Network

People can use the Ethereum network to develop applications across a wide range of industries and services. However, developers are exploring a new field, so it can be difficult to figure out the applications that will succeed or fail. Below are some interesting applications that are presently in the Ethereum network:

- Augur – This open-source application is designed to predict events and receive rewards for correct forecasts. Predictions on future real world events such as who will become the next US President, are implemented through virtual shares. When a user purchases shares in a winning prediction, they can receive monetary rewards.

• Provenance – This application harnesses the power of the Ethereum network to improve the transparency of opaque supply chains. By keeping the origins and record of products, the project can build an accessible and open framework of information so consumers could make informed decisions when they purchase products.

• BlockApps – Provides an easy platform for businesses to build, manage, and use blockchain applications. From integration with legacy systems to full production and proof of concept, this app offers all the tools needed to develop private, semi-private, and public industry-specific blockchain apps.

• Uport – This application provides users with a convenient and secure way to take charge of personal information online. Users can control who can access and use their personal information instead of depending on government agencies or entrusting their personal data to third parties.

• Weifund – This open application provides an easy platform for crowdfunding campaigns that harness the power of smart contracts. It allows contributions to be converted into contractual-based digital assets, which could be used or traded inside the Ethereum platform.

The 2016 DAO Attack

At this point, you should already know the fact that the Ethereum network can be used to build DAOs. Well, in 2016, a DAO has been compromised due to a hacking attack. A startup company developed a DAO to provide a humanless venture capital service, which aims to help investors make decisions through the aid of smart contracts. The DAO was financed via an ICO and ended up raising about $150 Million from investors around the world.

Upon raising funds, The DAO software was hacked by cyber criminals who took Ether worth around $50 Million during that time. Although the negligence was not on the side of the Ethereum platform but because of the technical flaw in the system of DAO software, the executives of Ethereum were obliged to address the mess created by the attack.

After all the discussions, the Ethereum community came to an agreement to recover $50 million dollars' worth of Ether by making a change in the code – a process also known as a hard fork. The change in code moved the robbed funds to a fresh smart contract created to allow the original owners to draw back their tokens. However, the ramification of this decision is still controversial and debatable.

Ethereum is based on the blockchain network wherein every action recorded is irrevocable and permanent. By changing a code and writing the rules by which blockchains operate, Ethereum made a risky precedent that contradicts the very purpose of blockchain. If blockchain is modified every time a huge amount of money is involved or a number of users get affected, the major value proposition of blockchain (secure, anonymous, tamper-proof, and unchangeable) will be lost

While a fork was put forth, the Ethereum community and its executives were trapped in a perilous situation. If they failed to recover the robbed fund of the investors, trust in Ethereum could be lost. On the other side, retrieving the fund of the investors set actions that go against the main essence of decentralization and require a risky precedent.

At end of the day, the Ethereum Community came to a consensus to execute the hard fork and recover the stolen funds of DAO investors. But not all agreed with their decision. This lead to a division, creating the two parallel blockchains that now exist.

Ethereum Classic (ETC) is available for those who went against the hard fork. Ethereum (ETH) is available for most members of the network who voted yes to change a minor part of the blockchain and issue a refund to the rightful owners.

Ethereum Classic and Ethereum both have similar features and are essentially the same in every way, up to a certain part where the blockchain was rewritten or changed. This only shows that all that occurred on Ethereum up until the change in code is still valid on the Ethereum Classic blockchain. From the part where the hard fork was performed onwards, the two blockchains work separately.

Despite the controversies from the DAO software hack, Ethereum is still looking forward to big opportunities. By giving a user-friendly platform that allows users to equip the functions of blockchain technology, it is now helping in quickening the decentralization of the world economy. Apps that went through decentralization have the possibility to completely disrupt entire industries such as insurance, academia, real estate, health care, finance, and many more.

Chapter 4 - What is Ethereum Mining?

Currently, miners play a vital role in making Ethereum work effectively. Although, this role is not really obvious.

Many people assume that the essence of mining is to provide Ethereum tokens in a manner that does not stand in need of a central issuer. It's actually correct. At a rate of 5 tokens for every block mined, Ethers are obtained through the process of mining. However mining also has other important roles aside from generating the cryptocurrency.

Oftentimes, banks are responsible of storing accurate records of transactions. Banks make sure that money is not produced out of nowhere, and the people don't pay out their money more than once.

Although blockchains introduced a totally new form of storing records, one where the whole web (instead of an intermediary) confirms transactions and records them to the public ledger. While a 'trustless' financial system is the objective, somebody still requires to secure the financial data to preserve the accuracy of records.

One innovation that makes decentralized registration possible is mining.

Miners agree about the transaction record while avoiding fraud or cheats – an issue that had not been addressed in decentralized currencies before proof-of-work blockchains.

Ethereum, though, is finding other means of coming to an agreement about the genuineness of transactions – and mining is what's presently controlling the platform.

How Ethereum Mining Works

Ethereum and Bitcoin have almost identical mining processes.

In every block of transaction, miners utilize computers to frequently and immediately guess answers to a puzzle until someone wins.

The miners will operate the group's unique header metadata (like software version and timestamp) with a mixed-up function, only modifying the node value which affects the outcome of the hash value.

The miner will gain Ether upon finding a hash compatible with the current target. They will announce the block all over the network for every node to confirm and record to their own copy of the ledger. For example, if miner B discovers the hash, miner A will pause from processing on the current block and repeat the course for the next block.

It's hard for miners to cheat the process. It is impossible to fake this game and get the right puzzle answer. That is the reason why the puzzle-solving method is referred as 'proof-of-work'. On the other hand, it's so easy for other miners to confirm that the hash value is right.

Ideally, a miner recovers a block within 12 to 15 seconds. The algorithm will immediately change the problem's level of difficulty if this timeframe isn't being maintained. The miners randomly obtain Ether tokens and their gains rely on luck and the volume of computing power they allotted to it.

Ethash is a specialized proof-of-work algorithm that Ethereum is currently using. This algorithm demands massive memory, making it more difficult to mine utilizing costly Application-Specific Integrated Circuits (ASICs), which are designed especially for mining and are currently the sole profitable means of mining bitcoin.

In essence, it might have succeeded in that objective, since there is no available ASICs to mine Ethereum. Moreover, because Ethereum aims to shift from proof-of-work to proof-of-stake (which you will later learn), using an ASIC may not be an ideal option because it may not prove useful for long.

Top Benefits of Mining Ether

While it's proven that mining Ethereum is cost-effective, it might not be a smart option for those who simply want to obtain the currency. It's better for them to focus on buying Ethereum. Still, is it profitable to mine Ethereum? The answer is yes. Certainly, you can obtain Ethereum with low-power Graphics Processing Units (GPUs). Despite this, the price of Ethereum is still increasing.

It is projected that with a GPU (specifically Radeon R9-295-X2), you can possibly earn over $1,000 for every card each year, which shows that you can still break even before the year ends and start earning passively.

Because Ethereum's value is gradually increasing, your income margin will definitely increase even more. In many ways, the Ethereum network is similar to the Bitcoin network. However, it has two primary distinctions that are crucial for its progress: smart contracts and the shift to proof-of-stake.

Smart Contracts

Not similar to Bitcoin, the programming language used for writing Ethereum makes it more possible for developers to make 'programmable money' or smart contracts. The cryptocurrency world sees this as a revolutionary innovation and has paved the way for numerous opportunities to further develop the field.

Transition to Proof-of-Stake

The transition of Ethereum from proof-of-work (POW) to proof-of-stake (POS) is its second main distinction from Bitcoin. Understanding POW is crucial in order for you to understand POS.

The technology of blockchain was developed in 2009, the same year that Bitcoin was introduced. In this sense, blockchain can be considered as a kind of database and in the cryptocurrency world, the database of transaction is the blockchain. If a user tries to start a flawed transaction, the code of blockchain will detect that it is not valid and so will not permit its processing.

Basically, in mining a cryptocurrency like Ethereum, Litecoin, or Bitcoin, a user sets up a computer (or networks of computers) to answer the algorithm of the cryptocurrency.

The computers processing the transactions are doing extremely hard operations. Basically, the computer has to frequently check the code until it discovers the answer in order to confirm an acceptable transaction on a blockchain.

There are several flaws in the proof-of-work scheme. This includes:

- A high amount of initial investment in purchasing costly computers
- This system consumes huge amounts of power for mining
- Electricity expenses are costly and could easily eat up your income

Electricity expense is a crucial factor you need to consider in Ethereum mining. The needed electricity cost to support all Ethereum miners can be higher compared to the total power cost of a small country. In the long run, this flaw will bring a huge problem. In the next few years, there will be an increase in the power needed to mine.

Proof of Stake (POS)

By shifting into POS, you can already monitor the coins that you have using your wallet or your computer. For instance, if the network has 500 tokens and you stake 50 of your total coins, you will gain 10 percent of the deposits being staked. Therefore you will gain 10 percent of the total tokens from the platform. Instead of mining coins, you're staking it – and in doing so, you are actually locking your coins.

If you forge any transactions or if you don't confirm it, you will lose the tokens you locked in the networks.

The Benefits of POS

Electricity is not needed in POS, as the GPUs don't need to perform any cryptographic hashes. It has eliminated the need to spend a lot of money on electricity or hardware. If your goal is to gain rewards, you need to secure your coins. With POW, you are actually using electricity to convert into coins. With POS, you are making coins out of coins.

Is Ethereum Mining Profitable?

Notwithstanding the use or relevance of the smart contracts, a lot of cryptocurrency advocates and stakeholders like the concept. This contributes to the increasing price of Ethereum.

There are clear long-term advantages when it comes to a POS system implemented in the Ethereum network. It will help in saving electricity. It can also eliminate or reduce the hardware expenses.

Nevertheless, mining will still become a lucrative venture in the next few years. The conversion to POS isn't common (yet it is leading its way to mainstream adoption), and we are still relying on Ethereum mining to confirm the transaction in the blockchains. POS and smart contracts will help boost and increase Ethereum's value, making it a highly profitable cryptocurrency to mine.

Chapter 5 - How to Mine Ethereum

You can use any PC to mine Ethereum, but never use light devices with underpowered GPUs (such as laptops). Ethereum mining using the CPU is not practical. It takes a longer period to complete the process, but the revenue is lower compared to expenses.

When it comes to mining, GPUs are better than CPUs – and GPUs are at least 200 times faster than a typical CPU. Do note though, that nVidia cards are slower compared to AMD cards. If you're familiar with these cards' mainstream applications, you're probably wondering why AMD's offerings are considered superior. After all, nVidia is deemed better in almost every application there is. This is due to the fact that the main mining program for Ether is implemented in OpenCL – a software framework fully supported by AMD's GPUs. While nVidia GPUs can still work with the open-source framework, they're actually optimized for CUDA (the company's own version of OpenCL).

Indeed it takes a high volume of electricity in order to mine Ether. If mining is executed efficiently, an increase in profits can be gained by selling Ether tokens.

To be sure of your plan's profitability, you might need to use specialized mining calculators. There are also Ethereum Mining mini-computers for determining profits.

The Ethereum Mining Process

Below is a simple process to set-up your Ethereum mining node and begin mining your first Ether token.

Step 1 - Download Geth

The first thing that you need to do is establish your communication channel. You need to download a software called Geth. This will create a secure connection to the Ethereum network across the world while it coordinates your hardware. It'll provide updates on the processes being done, particularly those that need response from your end.

Geth is often downloaded as a Zip file, which you'll have to extract somewhere. It is ideal to use your C drive for this step. Use the Windows search option to look for CMD. If you are not certain, then you can browse around the search listing.

Step 2 - Locate Geth

The placeholder for the username is often similar to the system name (e.g. C:\Users\Username>). In locating Geth, you need to type in *cd/* in cmd. This is a command to shift directory. *C:\>* should be on highlight, which shows that you are in drive C.

Step 3 - Create an Account

At this point, you should start creating your user account. To do this, start by making a call: type in *geth account new* then press Enter. *C:\>geth account new* should be displayed now in the command prompt. This step also involves setting up your password. You need to be cautious in setting your password, and be sure that you use a strong combination of alphanumeric keys. After keying in the password, press Enter and you now have a new account.

Step 4 - Download Ethereum Blockchain

Linking the Geth to the Ethereum network is needed before it becomes functional. Type in *geth — RPC* on the command terminal before pressing the Enter key. This activity begins with downloading the Ethereum blockchain and linking with the world's blockchain. This action is time consuming and relies on the size of the blockchain. It also relies on your web connection speed. Be sure to wait until it's done before proceeding.

Step 5 - Install Ethminer

Now, you need to install a program that will allow the GPU to operate the blockchain algorithm needed in the Ethereum network. The ideal option for this difficult task is Ethminer. Create a fresh terminal for command then access the terminal icon (active) that is located on the taskbar before accessing the terminal window in the menu.

In the newly opened terminal window, put *cd prog* then press tab. *C:\>cd prog* must appear in the window, press tab to show *C:/> cd "Program Files"* then press Enter to display *C:\Program Files>*.

Type *cd cpp* and press Enter in order to proceed to the Ethereum mining folder. The terminal window will show *C:\Program Files\cpp-ethereum>* right after you press tab again.

Step 6 - Start Mining

Key in *Ethminer –G* on your terminal window then press the Enter key in order to start mining with your GPU. This will start Ethereum mining after the Directed Acyclic Graph (DAG) gets created. It's a huge file mainly kept in your

GPU's RAM so it can be compatible with ASIC. Nonetheless, you have to ensure that your HDD has sufficient space before doing this step.

If necessary, mining Ether using a CPU is also possible. Just type *ETHMINER* then push the Enter key to initiate the mining process. The creation of DAG is necessary in this phase, after which the connection with Ethminer will be taken over by Geth.

Chapter 6 - Investing in Ethereum

Part of the massive popularity of cryptocurrencies in 2017 is Ethereum. It is a decentralized system, which disrupts the need for third-parties or banks in sending payments across the internet.

The total market value of cryptocurrencies increased to more than $200 billion. These alternative currencies even entered the mainstream with the introduction of the first Bitcoin Futures on the Chicago Board Options Exchange. So, here are some reasons why you should invest in Ethereum.

1. It is growing in popularity

In a span of two years, Ethereum managed to establish itself as one of the fastest growing digital currencies in the market, second only to the largest digital currency in the world. The idea of Ethereum was first proposed by a 19 year old, Vitalik Buterin, in 2013. Presently, millions of people have already obtained this currency, though many say that the idea of having third-party apps that can run on their network is its main attraction.

2. Ethereum's value is rising

Ether, the valuation of Ethereum's currency, has gradually increased these past months as people have started setting up their own cryptocurrency wallets. It has been used for public trades since 2016 and the release of Ether is only limited to eighteen million every twelve months. These days, it isn't surprising at all to see a single Ether being valued at more than 700 USD.

3. Ether could be the future of currency

Ethereum and other digital currencies have the capacity to innovate and transform the financial system, in the same way Airbnb and Uber have done in their own field. Confidence in conventional markets is low given the emergence of a financial crisis ten years ago, and people are now becoming more confident with what the online world has to offer.

4. You can trade on exchanges

It's a good thing to have options as there are numerous cryptocurrency exchanges that allow Ethereum on their platform. One of the most distinguished, Coinbase, faces competition from exchanges like the Buy Virtual Currency.

This new platform offers individual account managers and effective customer service – all while accepting almost every digital currency available.

5. You can already use ETH to pay for products and services

More and more businesses are starting to accept digital currency as payment. Also, as people become more comfortable with cryptocurrencies, it's to be expected that the number of organizations that will get involved with Ether will rise over the next few years. In fact, Overstock.com, an online retailer of furniture, bedding, and DIY, which is located near Salt Lake City, notified their customers that they are already accepting cryptocurrencies as payment.

Chapter 7 - How to Make Money Buying and Selling Ethereum

We could compare the current status of Ethereum to that of Bitcoin during its introduction in 2009. A man from Norway invested $27 worth of Bitcoins in 2009 and just stored it in his wallet. The next time he checked it, BTC's value had already skyrocketed to $800,000 based on the current price.

We cannot say what could happen to Ethereum after a decade, but there is a big possibility that Ethereum will outgrow Bitcoin.

Purchasing Ether Tokens for Long-term Investment

The blockchain technology, which is the underlying technology of Ethereum, can be used for different purposes built in a system that is both decentralized and autonomous from the network. It can be a groundbreaking innovation that has the power to change the landscape in many industries.

The value of Ether will continue to hike thanks to the increasing demand for the Ethereum platform and its smart contracts. The platform experienced organic growth without any danger of massive spikes, and stability is no longer an issue. The movement in the demand and price of a specific digital currency can be seen as a metric of its potential.

The developers behind the success of Ethereum like to see the web as huge global computer that helps apps operate. This is probably the reason why more investors (including Bill Gates) are supporting the project.

Paving its way to a more stable industry: Microsoft Corporation is now offering blockchain as a service. Other big companies such as IBM have already expressed their willingness to cooperate. Meanwhile, researchers from the Massachusetts Institute of Technology (MIT) are also doing active study and even offering their own alternatives to the Ethereum blockchain.

At present, Ethereum is the second largest cryptocurrency in terms of market capitalization. It's also among the leading cryptocurrencies when it comes to volume and popularity.

How and Where to Buy Ethereum

Numerous online platforms can be used to purchase digital currencies such as Ethereum. Among them is Coinbase, which is noted as a reliable and secure platform for buying and selling Ether tokens. Coinbase can be used in over

30 countries around the world including Switzerland, San Marino, Slovakia, Slovenia, Spain, Sweden, Singapore, Canada, United States, United Kingdom, Romania, Portugal, Poland, Norway, Austria, Netherlands, Belgium, Monaco, Bulgaria, Malta, Croatia, Liechtenstein, Cyprus, Latvia, Czech republic, Italy, Denmark, Ireland, Finland, Hungary, France, and Greece.

In 2017, Coinbase has become the world's biggest Bitcoin dealer. It is now possible to invest in Ethereum and Bitcoin using your bank account or through other payment methods such as Interact Online and SEPA transfer.

In Coinbase, buyers can easily purchase or sell digital currencies of their choice. It's so user-friendly that it is possible for the users to purchase Ethereum and Bitcoin instantly with a debit card or credit card.

In case you are still in doubt if it is really reliable, Coinbase is located in California and is supported by institutional investors and venture capitalists.

Here are the steps on how to set up a Coinbase account

Step 1 - The first thing you need to do is sign up for a Coinbase account, so you can have a secure place where you can store your digital currency and exchange your fiat currency into cryptocurrencies.

Step 2 - After signing up, link a valid bank account, debit card, or credit card to the platform. You just need to complete a simple verification process so you can start using your account.

Step 3 - After buying your first digital currency, the platform will fulfill the process of purchasing and delivering your Ether tokens. The value of Ether varies over time. The price may go up or down, so Coinbase will update you of the prevailing exchange rate before you confirm the transaction.

These days, Ether's value when converted to fiat currency might be high but this could still be the ideal time to get involved in the trade – especially if you take a closer look at Ethereum's price chart.

Is It Possible to Make Money in Ethereum in Just An Hour?

Actually, yes. With the right knowledge, skills, and equipment, thousands of people have already made money from buying and selling Ether tokens. A small movement in the market can bring thousands of dollars into your pocket.

After setting up your account with Bitcoin exchanges such as Coinbase, you can start buying Ether tokens. Take note that there is no need to buy tokens in full units. You can purchase tokens even in fractions at present prices. This makes cryptocurrencies such as Ether easy targets for speculation.

Most cryptocurrency exchanges such as Coinbase don't charge for transferring the digital currency from one user to another, which is the main concept of the blockchain technology. However, if you like to send money to your bank account, the exchange will charge a minimal conversion fee, which is usually 3.99% if you are using a debit or credit card or 1.49% if you are using bank account. So try to stay away from using credit cards unless you can receive enough reward points to offset the expensive charges.

After trading some Ether tokens in Coinbase, you can choose to level up to the bigger platforms such as the Global Digital Asset Exchange (GDAX), which is the Coinbase's advanced day trading service. You can use the same credentials with Coinbase, and you can easily send the digital tokens between the platforms that can really provide convenience. GDAX offers an interactive interface with real-time pricing data, a simplified buy-sell order process, as well as trade history, charting tools, and order book features.

Most day traders who are already comfortable with GDAX have completely stopped day trading through Coinbase's primary platform. GDAX also charges cheaper transaction fees compared to Coinbase, which range between 0.1% and 0.25% for buyers and surprisingly no charge for sellers. But take note that fees vary according to the monthly trade volume.

The primary benefit of the Coinbase system is that it provides a simpler interface and the order is guaranteed to fill, in exchange for a higher fee. Sellers don't need to pay any charges on GDAX, but there is a risk that the order may not be filled and you have to work on a new set price.

Learn How to Read Charts and Look for Trends

If you are convinced that the cryptocurrency market will increase in value in the near future, then your strategy is to collect as much as coins as you can. Include the right cryptocurrencies to diversify your portfolio so you can make money over time.

One strategy to do this is to purchase tokens during a downtrend and allow the profits to roll over. It is best to enter and exit positions slowly in case the trend behaves contrary to market prediction. Stay away from trading in huge emotional or reactionary swings and avoid trading several times a week so you can minimize your fees.

Another way to determine if the Ether stock price is undervalued or overvalued is by reading the moving averages, which you can find on the stock charts. This will help in smoothing out volatility and figuring out the direction of Ether.

More often than not, short-term moving averages (usually represented in red line) can cross over long-term moving averages (usually represented in black line). This is usually succeeded with a spike in the price movement. You must also take a closer look at the spikes in the trade volume, as this could indicate great sentiments of excitement or fear in the market.

Chapter 8 - Ethereum and Other Cryptocurrencies

Ethereum is now the second biggest cryptocurrency in the world, only next to Bitcoin. Some advocates even believe that this digital currency is well positioned to soon take over BTC.

However, it's a wise investment strategy to never put all your eggs in one basket. The classic method of diversification is still applicable when it comes to your cryptocurrency holdings. As such, it's necessary to learn about other cryptocurrencies that show potential.

Bitcoin Cash (BCH)

For a short period in the last quarter of 2017, disagreement rose among the adopters of Bitcoin over the technical restrictions of Bitcoin. This has resulted to a hard fork in the blockchain, which in turn resulted to the introduction of Bitcoin Cash (BCH).

Some disappointed cryptocurrency miners decided to fork the token by using a new software, with the primary objective of scaling the cryptocurrency. Since its introduction, the new token has secured its ranking among the top digital currencies, without the need to take over Bitcoin when it comes to buzz, value, and usage. BCH has an estimated market cap of more than $28 Billion.

Monero (XMR)

Another decentralized and open-source digital currency is the Monero. This private and untraceable currency was released in the first quarter of 2014.

In just a short period, it managed to generate interest within the cryptography community. It easily convinced countless traders and enthusiasts to invest. The progress of Monero is purely community-driven and donation-based.

This digital currency has been introduced to focus on scalability and decentralization. It allows extra security by applying a special cryptographic technique called "ring signatures". In this technique, a set of cryptographic signatures is shown (including the one which is the real participant), but since every signature in the set seems valid, the real one cannot be identified.

Cardano (ADA)

Originally, Cardano is a platform used for transferring digital currency. It facilitates storage and transfer of value through its ADA token. Like Ether, the network of Cardano aims to operate decentralized applications in the blockchain. The network was developed by a co-founder of the Ethereum Network, Charles Hopkins. It is also regarded as the Ethereum of Japan since around 95% of its ICOs were raised from the country. The network is currently administered by a global group of academics and scientists who specialize in blockchain applications. Cardano's market capitalization is estimated to be around $16 Billion.

Ripple (XRP)

Ripple is a cryptocurrency launched in 2012. It now has a market capitalization of $1.26 billion. The said digital currency is a real-time global settlement network that gives immediate, certain, and affordable international payments. It enables banking organizations and similar financial institutions to manage payments across geographical borders in near real-time (if not real-time) at a very low cost.

Ripple's structure doesn't require mining using GPU or CPU, thereby it decreases dependency on computational capacity and reduces network latency. Ripple's developers insist that dispensing price is an effective method of rewarding particular behaviors and so, they're planning to distribute the tokens through deals and institutional investments.

Dash (DASH)

A more secretive version of Bitcoin was launched in the first quarter of 2014. The Dash (also known as Darkcoin) was created and developed by Evan Duffield. In 2015, Darkcoin was renamed to Dash which means Digital Cash. It can be mined using a GPU or CPU.

The change on its name did not affect any of its technological features like InstantX and Darksend, It still gives anonymity as it executes on a decentralized mastercode web that makes transactions almost untraceable. Dash is now being used by a lot people around the globe.

Zcash (ZEC)

In the last quarter of 2016, an open-source and decentralized digital currency was released. It was the Zcash. It was referred to as the https of money, while Bitcoin was considered the http. Zcash gives privacy and selective transparency in all transactions.

Hence, Zcash still claims to give extra security wherein every transaction is noted and issued on a blockchain, but information such as the recipient, sender, and the amount is not indicated. "Shielded" transactions are being offered by this digital currency, which permit the content to be encrypted utilizing new cryptographic methods. The cryptographic technique called zk-SNARK is a zero-knowledge proof construction – this was developed by the same people behind Zcash.

Stellar (XLM)

XLM is now a major digital currency thanks to its staggering 29,400% growth last year. The XLM token is a breakaway token from Ripple and was introduced in 2014 by Jed McCaleb – a co-founder of Ripple and Jouce Kim (a former lawyer) after an internal disagreement in the Ripple network. Similar to Ripple, Stellar is a transaction platform that offers easy and fast international money transfer. Its market capitalization is estimated to be around $10.5 Billion.

Litecoin (LTC)

Released in 2011, Litecoin is one of the first digital currencies that came out after the birth of Bitcoin. Litecoin is often referred to as the silver of the cryptocurrency world. The man behind the creation of Litecoin, Charlie Lee is a graduate from Massachusetts Institute of Technology (MIT) and a former engineer at Google.

The said digital currency is patterned on an open-source global payment web that's not owned by any central authority or third party. Just like some digital currencies, it also utilizes "scrypt" as proof-of-work. Even though Litecoin is similar to Bitcoin in many ways, Litecoin has a faster rate of block generation and therefore, gives immediate transaction confirmation. Many investors (aside from developers) are now embracing LTC.

Chapter 9 - The Future of Ethereum

In the past two years, digital currencies have attracted the attention of many investors, particularly after the historic rise in popularity of digital currencies such as Ether and Bitcoin. For instance, in the latter part of 2015, a single BTC was only worth around $440, while BTC was worth around $3000 in July 2017 – and has increased to around $8,000 in November 2017.

Cryptocurrency investors project that the price of Ether can go beyond $5,000 before 2018 ends. Its price was only $10 in 2017, and now it's around $800. Of course, there are those skeptical of this prediction. Take note that in order to reach $2,000, the market cap of Ethereum should be $200 billion, and some suggest that it could even reach $2,000 in just one day.

Other investment experts also believe that Ether could reach $1,000 in value in 2020. This is seen as a very conservative estimate for the cryptocurrency. Experts are considering three main factors in forecasting price:

- Ether's demand
- Ether's application
- Ether's supply (current and future)

The demand for Ether is mainly influenced by two things. First, its usage as a currency that is built on a blockchain with different uses, and second as a possible vehicle for investment that will keep on increasing its value.

For Ether's functionality, the technology behind smart contracts is what entices people most. But in light of recent events, the establishment of new applications on top of the Ethereum blockchain can also boost demand.

Ether's unique selling point (at least when compared to Bitcoin) is its capacity to use smart contracts, which as we have discussed in the early part of this book, are contracts that are instantly executed without the need for any human input the moment their terms are met.

However, the platform also allows developers to establish decentralized applications or dApps aside from the blockchain technology. It's interesting to note that the more apps are built, the more Ether tokens increase in value. Investment experts believe that in a span of five to seven years, we can expect a 20-fold increase in the number of decentralized blockchain applications.

At present, there are around 96 million Ether coins in circulation. Even though this number is likely to increase in the next two years, it will possibly experience a plateau after. This means that the programmers behind the Ethereum project need to ensure that the number of ETH tokens in circulation will stay constant.

Ethereum May Overtake Bitcoin

Again, some cryptocurrency experts believe that Ether's price could outperform Bitcoin. Hence, a dollar invested in Ether could provide a higher ROI compared to if it were put in BTC.

Although this may seem impossible to believe in the early weeks of 2018 looking at the price of Bitcoin, we are already aware that in the last weeks, BTC price fell down to $6,000. It is possible that Bitcoin is now used by investors for short-term revenue generation. It is also important to note that the assertion is based on the rise of Ethereum between 2015 and 2017, while the assertion for BTC was between 2009 and 2017.

As a matter of fact, Olaf Carlson Wee, the Chief Executive Officer (CEO) of Polychain Capital, believes that Ethereum's market capitalization can take over Bitcoin's in 2018. There are numerous indicators showing positive support for this projection.

Basically, Bitcoin has already lost around 50% of its market share to Ethereum in the past four months. It is also interesting to note that only four months ago, 90 percent of all funds invested in digital currency was poured into BTC.

But this number has dropped to around 45%, and the share of Ethereum has increased four-fold, which puts it around the 30 percent mark.

It's also helpful to know the backers of a currency to assess if Ether can really overtake Bitcoin. The focus of Bitcoin into payment processing makes it attractive with governments such as China and Japan.

However, the smart contract technology of Ethereum make it attractive among companies who have vested interest in actual applications. For instance, a new organization dubbed as the Enterprise Ethereum Alliance (EEA) has brought up the mission of fostering and facilitating Ether's growth.

EEA is composed of more than 86 companies that include Microsoft and JP Morgan. The support from these companies significantly affect the demand of the cryptocurrency and attests to its great potential.

However, Ethereum's future is not always on the positive end. In spite of the positive leaning of the market towards Ether, the digital currency is still facing major setbacks in nailing down its survival and growth.

Primarily, Ether may have several differences compared to Bitcoin, but it is still running on blockchain technology, which means it's also vulnerable to the problems that all present blockchain technologies are facing. One of the leading concerns is scalability.

In scalability, the main concern is whether the increased number of users can significantly affect the time of transaction. To put it simply, if more people are using the technology, there will be more transactions to register and place in the ledger.

This surge in the volume of transactions could mean that any transaction has to wait in a long queue before getting added into the block. As we have lightly discussed in the earlier chapters, this problem has created a fork problem, and there is no consensus yet on solving it.

Another concern with the Ethereum network is the probability of duplicating the technology. After all, any company could begin its own digital currency that's based on blockchain anytime. The main factor that grants value in any cryptocurrency is the agreement of the community in using a particular cryptocurrency.

Hence, it can be difficult to place full trust in one digital currency without the risk of another digital currency emerging and taking over the current standing of ETH and even BTC.

Of course, these concerns, when not solved, could jeopardize the future of Ether. Therefore, it makes any price projection for Ether in the next year or so quite difficult.

On the Matter of Security

As we've mentioned several times throughout the course of this book, more and more people are choosing to invest in Ether. Now with that trend, it's only to be expected that cyber criminals will be on the lookout for opportunities to earn big – taking advantage of every security vulnerability there is.

While hot wallets (online key storage solutions typically offered by cryptocurrency exchanges) may suffice for now, you'll still have to consider eventually transitioning to a cold wallet. Keep in mind that despite the convenience offered by hot wallets (being that they can be accessed anywhere as long as you're connected to the web), they're also the most vulnerable. In other words, since your wallet is on the internet, hackers from other parts of the world may end up getting your hard-earned Ether.

Cold wallets offer increased security simply by not relying on the web. They'll only be connected whenever you make a transaction. What are cold wallets exactly? They're USB devices designed specifically to function as a storage for cryptocurrency. Most of these physical wallets even come with backup solutions for complete peace of mind.

Despite being quite impressive, cold wallets (like the Ledger Nano S) are far from perfect. For one, finding one won't be easy – they're in limited supply, and the number of people interested in Ether is continuously increasing. Clearly, these devices are going to become more expensive as well.

Although some would say that you can always print a paper-based alternative (such as through MyEtherWallet), would you really want to risk losing everything if ever your cold wallet gets crumpled or smudged? It probably won't be worth it as a permanent solution, but it should be fine for temporary use.

Conclusion

Remember, investing in any opportunity could be good, or it may not. This is true not only for Ether but also in cryptocurrency in general, and of course on your perspective as the investor or day trader.

With digital currency still in its early years, the market remains quite volatile. Take note that although this book has provided you with the most relevant information available today, this is not a professional advice and doesn't guarantee results.

Still, it is important to note that there is a major upside in cryptocurrency investment. With the sector in its nascent stage, many investors are optimistic in projecting future prices – and that will make trading a nice venture.

Even if we say that Ether and other cryptocurrencies are still in a bubble, the trend can be very well be toward the digital current being an essential storage for value and medium of exchange. This is viable for those who are looking for a good long-term investment. While this could pose a high risk for day traders, it also comes with great rewards.

If you're in the US, take note that cryptocurrencies such as Ether are already legal – meaning they're already highly regulated. And when you hold it for investment, it is taxed similar to investment property. Hence, you can keep tab of your trades, and keep them as capital gains and then work with the tax office similar to any capital investment.

Meanwhile, the specific regulations are still not clear and could easily complicate things. For instance, it is not completely clear if the regulation for like-kind property is applicable for cryptocurrencies.

If they are applicable, this means that for each trade from one digital currency to another can be a taxable event for the year. If they are not applicable, then there's no need to pay the taxes on Ether holdings until you decide to cash them out. So, it will help you a lot to study the tax considerations in investing or holding Ether coins.

Regardless of what the future may hold, remember that the main focus of this book is to equip you with the knowledge you need so you can consider Ethereum as a possible (and viable) investment opportunity, whether for the long term or simply to make money in an hour.

Thank you and good luck!

www.ingramcontent.com/pod-product-compliance
Lightning Source LLC
Chambersburg PA
CBHW051321220526
45468CB00004B/1445